First World War
and Army of Occupation
War Diary
France, Belgium and Germany

60 DIVISION
Divisional Troops
3/3 London Field Company Royal Engineers
1 December 1915 - 30 November 1916

WO95/3028/3

The Naval & Military Press Ltd
www.nmarchive.com
Published in association with The National Archives

Published by

The Naval & Military Press Ltd

Unit 10 Ridgewood Industrial Park,

Uckfield, East Sussex,

TN22 5QE England

Tel: +44 (0) 1825 749494

www.naval-military-press.com

www.nmarchive.com

This diary has been reprinted in facsimile from the original. Any imperfections are inevitably reproduced and the quality may fall short of modern type and cartographic standards.

© **Crown Copyright**
Images reproduced by permission of The National Archives, London, England, 2015.

Contents

Document type	Place/Title	Date From	Date To
Heading	WO95/3028/3		
Heading	60th Division 3-3rd London Fld Coy R.E. 1915 Dec-1916 Nov To Salonika Re Numbered 522 (1917 Feb)		
Heading	War Diary Of 3/3rd London Field Coy. Royal Engineers 60th (London) Division. From 1st December 1915, To 31st December, 1915,		
War Diary	Bishops Stortford	01/12/1915	31/12/1915
War Diary	War Diary Of 3/3rd London Field Coy. Royal Engineers From 1st March. 1916, To 31st March, 1916.		
War Diary	Sutton Veny	01/03/1916	30/03/1916
Heading	War Diary Of 3/3rd London Field Company. Royal Engineers. From 1st April, 1916 To 30th April, 1916.		
War Diary	Sutton Veny	01/04/1916	30/04/1916
Miscellaneous	Appendix "A" 60th (London) Divisional Engineers.	01/04/1916	01/04/1916
Miscellaneous	Appendix "B" 60th (London) Divisional Engineers.	08/04/1916	08/04/1916
Miscellaneous	Appendix "C" 60th (London) Divisional Engineers.	15/04/1916	15/04/1916
Miscellaneous	Appendix "D" 60th (London) Divisional Engineers.	22/04/1916	22/04/1916
Miscellaneous	Appendix "E". 60th (London) Divisional Engineers.	29/04/1916	29/04/1916
War Diary	Sutton Veny	01/05/1916	31/05/1916
Miscellaneous	Programme Of Work For Week Ending 27th May 1916.	27/05/1916	27/05/1916
Miscellaneous	Programme Of Work For Week Ending 6th May, 1916.	06/05/1916	06/05/1916
Miscellaneous	Programme Of Work For Week Ending 13th May, 1916.	13/05/1916	13/05/1916
Miscellaneous	Programme Of Work For Week Ending 20th May, 1916.	20/05/1916	20/05/1916
Miscellaneous	Programme Of Work For Week Ending 3rd June 1916.	03/06/1916	03/06/1916
Heading	War Diary Of 3/3rd London Field Company, R.E. From 1st June 1916, To 21st June 1916.		
War Diary	Sutton Veny	01/06/1916	21/06/1916
Heading	War Diary Of 3/3rd. Lon. Field Coy. R.E. For The Period 21st. To 30th. June, 1916.		
War Diary	Warminster	21/06/1916	21/06/1916
War Diary	Southampton	21/06/1916	21/06/1916
War Diary	Havre	22/06/1916	23/06/1916
War Diary	St. Pol.	24/06/1916	24/06/1916
War Diary	Neuville-au-Cornet	24/06/1916	25/06/1916
War Diary	Louez	25/06/1916	27/06/1916
War Diary	Anzin	27/06/1916	30/06/1916
Heading	War Diary Of The 3/3rd London Field Coy Royal Engineers 1st-31st July 1916		
War Diary	Anzin	01/07/1916	31/07/1916
Heading	War Diary Of 3/3rd London Field Coy. R.E. August 1916		
War Diary	Anzin	01/08/1916	31/08/1916
Heading	War Diary Of 3/3rd. London Field Coy. R.E. 60th. London Divisional Engineers For 1st. To 30th. September, 1916		
War Diary	Anzin	01/09/1916	30/09/1916
Heading	War Diary Of 3/3rd London Field Coy R.E. 1st To 31st October 1916		

War Diary	Anzin	01/10/1916	24/10/1916
War Diary	Hermaville	24/10/1916	24/10/1916
War Diary	Ferme-Doffine	24/10/1916	25/10/1916
War Diary	Ivergny	25/10/1916	28/10/1916
War Diary	Occoches	28/10/1916	29/10/1916
War Diary	Famechon	29/10/1916	31/10/1916
War Diary	Coigneux	31/10/1916	31/10/1916
Heading	War Diary Of 3/3rd London Field Company. R.E. (T) November 1916		
War Diary	Coigneux	01/11/1916	02/11/1916
War Diary	Outrebois	02/11/1916	03/11/1916
War Diary	Saint Hilaire	04/11/1916	04/11/1916
War Diary	Brucamps	04/11/1916	25/11/1916
War Diary	Longpre	25/11/1916	25/11/1916
War Diary	St Julien-Du-Sault	26/11/1916	27/11/1916
War Diary	Marseilles	28/11/1916	29/11/1916
War Diary	Pointe Rouge	29/11/1916	30/11/1916
War Diary	Camp Musso	30/11/1916	30/11/1916
Heading	60th Division 60th Divl Signal Coy R.E.1915 Oct-1915 Dec 1916 Jun-1916 Nov		

WO 95/3028/3

60TH DIVISION

3-3RD LONDON FLD COY R.E.

~~JUN — NOV 1916~~

1915 DEC — 1916 NOV

TO SALONIKA
RE NUMBERED 522 (1917 FEB)

522 Coy

CONFIDENTIAL.

WAR DIARY of

3/3rd LONDON FIELD COY. ROYAL ENGINEERS

60th (LONDON) DIVISION.

From 1st December 1915, to 31st December, 1915.

Army Form C.2188.

WAR DIARY
of
3/3rd LONDON FIELD COY. ROYAL ENGINEERS.

Hour, Date, Place.		Summary of Events and Information.	Remarks and References to Appendices.
8.30 - 1. 6.30 - 10.30 p.m.	1-12-15. BISHOPS STORTFORD. "	Obstacles. Night operations.	wm
8.30 - 4.	2-12-15. "	Pontoon Bridging. Recruits - Squad Drill & musketry.	wm
9 - 4 p.m.	3-12-15. "	Route march.	wm
9 - 12.	4-12-15. "	Company drill. Inspection of clothing.	wm
9.30 a.m.	5-12-15. "	Church Parade.	wm
9 - 4 p.m.	6-12-15. "	Sapping, mining & explosives.	wm
6 - 7 p.m.	"	Lecture on Bombing.	wm
		O.C. presided at Court of Inquiry re accidents to mechanically propelled vehicles of 60th Divsl. Signal Coy.	
9 - 4 p.m. 6 - 7 p.m.	7-12-15. " "	Pontoon Bridging. Lecture on Demolitions.	wm
9 - 4.	8-12-15. "	Sapping, mining and bombing.	wm
9 - 4.	9-12-15. "	Route march and reconnaissance of R.ASH from CLAYGATE to HADHAM FORD. O.C. President at Court of Inquiry re loss of Technical Stores of 60th London Divsl. Signal Coy.	wm

Army Form C.2188.

Page 2.

WAR DIARY
of
3/3rd LONDON FIELD COY. ROYAL ENGINEERS.

Hour, Date, Place.			Summary of Events and Information.	Remarks and References to appendices.
9 – 1.	10-12-15.	BISHOPS STORTFORD.	Barbed wire entanglements. No. 2 Section working on magazine at Divsl. Bombing School.	
6.30 – 11 p.m.	"	"	Night operations - Entanglements and revetting.	
8.30 – 1.	11-12-15.	"	Company drill. O.C. proceeded on leave of absence to attend examinations of R.C.V.S.	
9.30 a.m.	12-12-15.	"	Church Parade.	
9 – 4.	13-12-15.	"	Sapping, mining and explosives.	
9 – 1. 2 – 4.	" "	" "	Recruits – musketry. Use of spars.	
9 – 4. 6 – 7 p.m.	14-12-15.	" "	Pontoon Bridging. Lecture on Trestle Bridging. LIEUT. WALKER proceeded to KELVEDON to collect explosives.	
9 – 1.	15-12-15.	"	Sapping, mining and bombing. Recruits – Field geometry. Night operation - obstacles and revetments.	

Army Form C.2188.

Page 3.

WAR DIARY

of

3/3rd LONDON FIELD COY. ROYAL ENGINEERS.

Hour, Date, Place.	Summary of Events and Information.	Remarks and References to Appendices.
9 - 4. 16-12-15. BISHOPS STORTFORD.	Route march and reconnaissance of R.ASH from HADHAM FORD to MUCH HADHAM FORD.	[initials]
8.30 - 1. 17-12-15. "	CAPT. MONCRIEFF and 2nd LIEUT.WILLCOCKS attended as members of Board to check Company stores. No.4 Section at work on Stables. Company - Entanglements. Night operations. Earthworks.	[initials]
9 - 12. 18-12-15. "	Company and saluting drill. O.C. returned from leave of absence.	[initials]
9.30 a.m. 19-12-15. "	Church Parade.	[initials]
8.30 - 1. 20-12-15. " 6 - 11 p.m. "	Pontoon Bridging. Night operations - obstacles and revetments.	[initials]
9 - 4. 21-12-15. " 6 - 7 p.m. "	Route march and road reconnaissance. Lecture on force pumps and water supply.	[initials]
8.30 - 4. 22-12-15. " 8.30 - 4. 23-12-15. "	Earthworks - Revetting and obstacles. Bombing.	[initials]
8.30 - 1. " 2 - 3 p.m. " 3 - 4 p.m. "	Recruits - Musketry. Field Geometry. Entanglements.	[initials]

Army Form C.2188.

Page 4.

WAR DIARY
of
3/3rd LONDON FIELD COY. ROYAL ENGINEERS.

Hour, Date, Place.		Summary of Events and Information.	Remarks and References to Appendices.
	23-12-15. BISHOP STORTFORD.	2nd LIEUT. KILLINGBACK attended as member of a Board to examine clothing of the 2/4th London Field Coy. R.E.	WJM
8.15 a.m.	24-12-15. BISHOP STORTFORD.	Company Parade.	WJM
9.30 a.m.	"	Inspection by G.O.C. 60th (LONDON) DIVISION.	
10.30 - 12.	"	Company Drill.	WJM
3 p.m.	"	Pay Parade.	
8.30 a.m.	25-12-15.	Check Parade.	
12 noon.	"	Dinner for men on week-end pass.) Xmas.	WJM
1.30 p.m.	"	Dinner for men not on week-end pass.)	
9.30 a.m.	26-12-15.	Church Parade.	
11 a.m.	"	Office Parade C.R.E.'s Office re Inspection held on 24-12-15.	WJM
9 a.m.	27-12-15.	Check Parade.	
		Holiday by permission, G.O.C.	
7. - 10.30p.m.	"	Concert; extension granted by G.O.C. men to be in Billets 11 p.m.	WJM
		Interviewed G.O.C. re roads in Stables &c.	

Army Form C.2188.

Page 5.

WAR DIARY
of
3/3rd LONDON FIELD COY. ROYAL ENGINEERS.

Hour, Date, Place.	Summary of Events and Information.	Remarks and References to Appendices.
9 – 5 p.m. 28-12-15. BISHOPS STORTFORD.	2 Sections, road repairs 2/7 ARTILLERY CAMP, STANSTED. 1 Section road repairs, SILVERLEYS. 40 Carpenters on gutters, SILVERLEYS. 1 Section removing tree from Road, HADHAM HALL.	ffm
8-15 – 5. 29-12-15. "	2 Sections R.F.A. GUN PARK; Road. 1 Section collecting brushwood. 1 Section removing tree, HADHAM HALL. 40 Carpenters on SILVERLEYS STABLES.	ffm
2.30 p.m. "	O.C. went with D.O.R.E. to SILVERLEYS and STANSTED CAMPS. Fatigue in gravel pit, LONDON SCOTTISH; 25. 1 Trestle wagon to Harlow for timber for Bombing School Cookhouse. 2nd LIEUT. CASE and 2nd LIEUT. WHYTE recommended higher rate of pay.	ffm
8.15 – 5 p.m. 30-12-15. "	2 Sections R.F.A. GUN PARK ROAD. 1 Section collecting brushwood. 1 Section road, SILVERLEYS. Limber wagon received.	ffm
8.15 – 5 p.m. 31-12-15. "	2 Sections R.F.A. GUN PARK, Road. 1 Section R.F.A. GUN PARK, Road. Fatigue party R.F.A. Gravel Pit. Much obstruction from Road Board's men at SILVERLEYS. 1 Section making Fascines.	ffm

Army Form C.2188.

Page 6.

WAR DIARY
of
3/3rd LONDON FIELD COY. ROYAL ENGINEERS.

Hour, Date, Place.	Summary of Events and Information.	Remarks and References to Appendices.
8.15 – 5 p.m. 31-12-15 BISHOPS STORTFORD. " "	2nd LIEUT. WHYTE proceeded to HARLOW to buy brushwood. LIEUT. WALKER and Batman proceeded to Newark, S.M.E. Water Cart received.	mm

W W Weelney
MAJOR.
O.O. 2/3rd LONDON FIELD Co. R.E.

C O N F I D E N T I A L.

WAR DIARY OF

3/3rd London Field Coy. Royal Engineers

from 1st March, 1916, to 31st March, 1916.

R.E. Camp.
Sutton Veny.

Army Form C. 2118.

WAR DIARY
or
INTELLIGENCE SUMMARY.
(Erase heading not required.)

Instructions regarding War Diaries and Intelligence Summaries are contained in F.S. Regs., Part II. and the Staff Manual respectively. Title pages will be prepared in manuscript.

Place	Date	Hour	Summary of Events and Information	Remarks and references to Appendices
	1916			
SUTTON VENY	1-3-16	7.30 a.m.	Physical drill.	Ult
		8.45 a.m.	Company on Divisional Entrenching Scheme. One Officer and 15 N.C.O.'s and men mining. Drivers exercising horses and musketry.	
do.	2-3-16	7.30 a.m.	Physical drill.	Ult
		8.45 a.m.	1 Officer and 12 N.C.O.'s mining. Remainder of Company on Divisional Entrenching Scheme. Drivers riding and driving drill. LIEUT. DUNNAGE reported from Course at BRIGHTLINGSEA.	
do.	3.3.16	7.30 a.m.	Physical Drill.	Ult
		8.45 a.m.	1 Officer and 2 N.C.O.'s at Rifle Ranges with party of infantry entrenching. Remainder of Company on Divisional Entrenching Scheme. No.2057 SAPPER SAXBY, H.E. proceeded to CLACTON-ON-SEA to HOME SERVICE DETAILS.	
		5.30 p.m.	Foot Inspection.	
do.	4.3.16	7.30 a.m.	Physical drill.	Ult
		8.45 a.m.	Company drill, drivers: Riding and driving drill. 2nd LIEUT. WHYTE proceeded to ALDERSHOT for a Course of Mounted Duties. No.2855, SAPPER STIFF,H., discharged under para.392 (vi) King's Regulations. No.2865, DRIVER AUSTIN, F.W. returned from a Course of Cold Shoeing at ROMSEY.	
Do.	5.3.16	10.40 a.m.	Church Parade. 2nd LIEUT. WILLCOCKS reported from Course in Mounted Duties, ALDERSHOT.	Ult

Army Form C. 2118.

WAR DIARY
or
INTELLIGENCE-SUMMARY.
(Erase heading not required.)

Instructions regarding War Diaries and Intelligence Summaries are contained in F. S. Regs., Part II. and the Staff Manual respectively. Title pages will be prepared in manuscript.

Place	Date	Hour	Summary of Events and Information	Remarks and references to Appendices
SUTTON VENY.	6.3.1916	7.30 a.m. 8.45 a.m.	Physical drill. 1 Officer and 2 N.C.O.'s entrenching scheme at RANGES. Remainder of Company on Divisional entrenching scheme at SUTTON VENY TRENCHES. Mounted Section exercising horses.	/llr
do.	7.3.1916	7.30 a.m. 8.45 a.m.	Physical drill. 1 Officer, 1 N.C.O's and 12 sappers Mining. Remainder of Company Divisional entrenching scheme, SUTTON VENY TRENCHES. CAPTAIN MONCRIEFF proceeded on sick leave. Mounted Section exercising horses.	/llr
do.	8.3.1916	7.30 a.m. 8.45 a.m.	Physical drill. Company employed on Divisional entrenchments at SUTTON VENY TRENCHES. Mounted Section exercising horses. MAJOR W.S.MULVEY left to take over appointment at RIPON.	/llr
do.	9.3.1916.	7.30 a.m. 8.45 a.m.	Physical drill. Company on Divisional Entrenching scheme. Drivers riding and driving drill.	/llr
do.	10.3.1916.	7.30 a.m. 8.45 a.m.	Physical drill. Company on Divisional Entrenching Scheme. 2nd LIEUT. CASE and 2 N.C.O.'s on work at Ranges. Drivers exercising horses.	/llr

1577 Wt.W10791/1773 500,000 1/15 D.D.&L. ADSS./Forms/C. 2118.

Army Form C. 2118.

WAR DIARY
INTELLIGENCE SUMMARY.
(Erase heading not required.)

Instructions regarding War Diaries and Intelligence Summaries are contained in F.S. Regs., Part II. and the Staff Manual respectively. Title pages will be prepared in manuscript.

Place	Date	Hour	Summary of Events and Information	Remarks and references to Appendices
SUTTON VENY.	11.3.1916.	7.30 a.m.	Physical drill.	
		8.45 a.m.	Company drill.	
			Drivers exercising horses.	
do.	12.3.1916.	10.45 a.m.	Company found Camp Fatigues. Church Parade. Fatigue party proceeded to HORNINGSHAM for faggots.	
do.	13.3.1916.	7 a.m.	Company on Musketry Course, SUTTON VENY RANGES. 2nd LIEUT. WILLCOCKS on Divisional Entrenching Scheme, SUTTON VENY TRENCHES. 2nd LIEUT. JAMESON and 2 N.C.O.'s on Works at Range.	
do.	14.3.1916.	7 a.m.	Company on Musketry Course. 2nd LIEUT. WILLCOCKS at SUTTON VENY TRENCHES. LIEUT. DUNNAGE on works at Range. 2 Officers and 2 N.C.O.'s attended anti-gas Lect. res at No. 4 Camp.	
do.	15.3.1916.	7 a.m.	Company at Musketry Course SUTTON VENY RANGES, and found Camp duties. 2nd LIEUT. WILLCOCKS on entrenching Scheme, SUTTON VENY TRENCHES. LIEUT. DUNNAGE on works at ranges.	
do.	16.3.1916.	7 a.m.	Company on Musketry Course, SUTTON VENY RANGES. 2nd LIEUT. CASE and party on entrenching scheme, SUTTON VENY TRENCHES. LIEUT. DUNNAGE at works on Ranges. Drivers riding and driving drill.	
do.	17.3.1916.	7 a.m.	Company on Musketry Course, SUTTON VENY RANGES. Divisional Engineers practice alarm. Drivers riding and driving drill.	

Army Form C. 2118.

WAR DIARY
of
INTELLIGENCE SUMMARY.
(Erase heading not required.)

Instructions regarding War Diaries and Intelligence Summaries are contained in F. S. Regs., Part II. and the Staff Manual respectively. Title pages will be prepared in manuscript.

Place	Date	Hour	Summary of Events and Information	Remarks and references to Appendices
SUTTON VENY	18.3.1916.	7.30 a.m.	Details on Musketry Course. 2nd LIEUT. JAMESON and party at work on ranges. Remainder of Company on Divisional Entrenching scheme. Drivers riding and driving drill.	
do.	19.3.1916.	10.45 a.m.	Church Parade.	
do.	20.3.1916.	7.30 a.m.	Physical Drill. 2nd LIEUT. WILLCOCKS and party on Divisional Entrenching Scheme. Remainder of Company demolitions and mining.	
		2 p.m.	Lecture by LIEUT. WALKER on demolitions (weather inclement). CAPT. MONCRIEFF returned from sick leave.	
do.	21.3.1916.	7.30 a.m.	Physical drill. 2nd LIEUT. CASE and party on Divisional entrenching Scheme. Remainder of Company on trip wires and automatic alarms.	
		2 p.m.	Company on camp fatigues. Earthworks.	
do.	22.3.1916.	7.30 a.m.	Physical drill. 2nd LIEUT. THOMAS and party on Divisional entrenching Scheme. Remainder of Company on trip wires and automatic alarms.	
do.	23.3.1916.	6.30 a.m.	Fatigue parade. Cleaning and loading wagons.	
		8.40 a.m.	Route march.	

Army Form C. 2118.

WAR DIARY
or
INTELLIGENCE-SUMMARY.
(Erase heading not required.)

Instructions regarding War Diaries and Intelligence Summaries are contained in F. S. Regs., Part II. and the Staff Manual respectively. Title pages will be prepared in manuscript.

Place	Date	Hour	Summary of Events and Information	Remarks and references to Appendices
SUTTON VENY.	23.3.1916.	2 p.m.	Earthworks, bombing and demolitions.	/h
do.	24.3.1916.	7.30 a.m.	Physical drill.	/h
		8.45 a.m.	2nd LIEUT. WILLCOCKS and party on Divisional Entrenching scheme, Company on Camp fatigues and automatic alarms.	
		2 p.m.	Earthworks, bombing and automatic alarms.	
do.	25.3.1916.	7.30 a.m.	Physical drill.	/h
		9 a.m.	Bayonet fighting, squad and section drill. 2nd LIEUT. JAMESON reported for duty from ALDERSHOT. 2nd LIEUT. CASE proceeded to ALDERSHOT.	
do.	26.3.1916.	10.30 a.m.	Church Parade.	/h
do.	27.3.1916.	7.30 a.m.	Physical drill.	/h
		8.45 a.m.	2nd LIEUT. JAMESON and party on entrenching scheme. Rest of Company on mining and revetting. Company on camp fatigues. Earthworks.	
do.	28.3.1916.	7.30 a.m.	Loading pontoon wagons.	/h
		9 - 4 p.m.	Lecture and practical demonstrations on "Explosives and their uses" by LIEUT. WALKER.	

O.C. 2/8TH LONDON FIELD Co. R.E.

Army Form C. 2118.

WAR DIARY
or
INTELLIGENCE SUMMARY.
(Erase heading not required.)

Instructions regarding War Diaries and Intelligence Summaries are contained in F.S. Regs., Part II. and the Staff Manual respectively. Title pages will be prepared in manuscript.

Place	Date	Hour	Summary of Events and Information	Remarks and references to Appendices
SUTTON VENY	29.3.1916	7.30 a.m.	Physical drill.	
		8.45 a.m.	2nd LIEUT. JAMESON and party on entrenching Scheme. Rest of Company on automatic alarms and wire entanglements.	/h
do.	30.3.1916	7.30 a.m.	Physical drill.	/h
		8.45 a.m.	Route march. SUTTON VENY, CROCKERTON GREEN, LONGBRIDGE DEVERILL, SUTTON VENY. 2nd LIEUT. JAMESON and party on entrenching Scheme.	/h
		8.30 p.m.	Earthworks and entanglements, Sutton Veny Trenches.	

1577 Wt.W10791/1773 500,000 1/15 D.D. & L. A.D.S.S./Forms/C. 2118.

CONFIDENTIAL.

WAR DIARY OF

3/3rd LONDON FIELD COMPANY, ROYAL ENGINEERS.

from 1st April, 1916 to 30th April, 1916.

RECEIVED BY
2 1 JUN 1916
T.F. RECORDS, LONDON

Army Form C. 2118.

WAR DIARY
or
INTELLIGENCE SUMMARY.
(Erase heading not required.)

Instructions regarding War Diaries and Intelligence Summaries are contained in F. S. Regs., Part II. and the Staff Manual respectively. Title pages will be prepared in manuscript.

Place	Date	Hour	Summary of Events and Information	Remarks and references to Appendices
Sutton Veny	April 1.	7.30 a.m.	Physical drill.	
		9 a.m.	Bayonet fighting, squad and section drill and kit inspection.	/Mr
		10 a.m.	Horse and harness inspection.	
			Wire breakers and reflectors received.	/Mr
	2.	10.45.	Church Parade.	/Mr
	3.	7.30.	Physical drill.	
		9 a.m.	Earthworks and Mining. Infantry instruction.	
		2 p.m.	Company drill.	
		8.30 p.m.	Demolitions, flares and automatic alarms.	/Mr
	4.	7.30.	Physical drill.	
		9 a.m.	Earthworks and pontooning. Infantry instruction. 2nd LIEUT. M.E. THOMAS relinquished Commission.	/Mr
	5.	7.5 a.m.	Emergency alarm, ready to move off 7.45 a.m.	
		9 a.m.	Earthworks, demolitions and automatic alarms. Infantry instruction. Camp orderly duties. LIEUT. C.E. DUNNAGE proceeded on 7 days sick leave. 60 fathoms of 3" cordage received.	/Mr
	6.	7.30	Physical drill.	
		9 a.m.	Earthworks. Infantry instruction. Knotting and lashing.	/Mr

1577 Wt. W10791/1773 500,000 1/15 D.D.&L. A.D.S.S./Forms/C. 2118.

Army Form C. 2118.

WAR DIARY
or
INTELLIGENCE SUMMARY.
(Erase heading not required.)

Instructions regarding War Diaries and Intelligence
Summaries are contained in F. S. Regs., Part II.
and the Staff Manual respectively. Title pages
will be prepared in manuscript.

Place	Date	Hour	Summary of Events and Information	Remarks and references to Appendices
Sutton Veny	April 6	11 a.m.	Route march and road reconnaissance. Route: SUTTON VENY, KNOOK, CORTON, SUTTON VENY.	/s/
	7	7.30	Physical drill	/s/
		9 a.m.	Earthworks and demolitions.	
		9.30 p.m.	Foot inspection.	
	8	7.30	Physical drill.	/s/
		9 a.m.	Bayonet fighting, squad and section drill.	/s/
			Camp orderly duties.	
	9	10.30	Church Parade.	
	10.	7.30	Physical drill.	
		9 a.m.	Earthworks, mining and company drill. Infantry instruction.	/s/
		8.30 p.m.	Entanglements and earthworks by night. Infantry instruction.	
	11.	7.30	Physical drill.	
		9 a.m.	Earthworks and entanglements. Camp fatigues. Infantry instruction.	
		2.30	Inspection of vehicles and horses by BRIGADIER-GENERAL ROPER, R.E.	

Arthur [illegible] Capt.
O.C. R.E.

1577 Wt. W10791/1773 500,000 1/15 D. D. & L. A.D.S.S./Forms/C. 2118.

Army Form C. 2118.

WAR DIARY
or
INTELLIGENCE SUMMARY.
(Erase heading not required.)

Instructions regarding War Diaries and Intelligence Summaries are contained in F. S. Regs., Part II. and the Staff Manual respectively. Title pages will be prepared in manuscript.

Place	Date	Hour	Summary of Events and Information	Remarks and references to Appendices
Sutton Veny	April 11	7 p.m.	Emergency alarm. Ready to move off at 7.46 p.m.	Alu.
	12	8 p.m.	Infantry instruction.	
		7.30	Physical drill.	
	13	9 a.m.	Pontooning. Infantry instruction.	Alu.
		8 p.m.	Infantry instruction.	
		7 a.m.	Physical drill.	
		9 a.m.	Knotting and lashing. Infantry instruction.	Alu.
		11 a.m.	Section route march, meeting at a point and joining up.	
			LIEUT. G.E. DUNNAGE transferred to Third Line.	
	14		Draught saddlery received.	Alu.
		8 p.m.	Infantry instruction.	
		7 a.m.	Physical drill and saluting drill.	
		9 a.m.	Camp fatigues.	
		4 p.m.	Pay parade.	
		8 p.m.	Infantry instruction.	
		9.30 p.m.	Foot inspection.	
	15	7 a.m.	Physical drill.	Alu.
		9 a.m.	Kit inspection.	
	"	10 a.m.	Bayonet fighting and physical drill.	
			2nd LIEUT. R.C. CASE returned from ALDERSHOT Course.	

Army Form C. 2118.

WAR DIARY
~~INTELLIGENCE~~ SUMMARY.
(Erase heading not required.)

Instructions regarding War Diaries and Intelligence Summaries are contained in F. S. Regs., Part II. and the Staff Manual respectively. Title pages will be prepared in manuscript.

Place	Date	Hour	Summary of Events and Information	Remarks and references to Appendices
Sutton Veny	April 16	10.45 a.m.	Church Parade.	
	17	7 a.m.	Rifles and bayonets received.	
		9 a.m.	Physical drill.	
		7.30 p.m.	Infantry instruction and earthworks.	
		2 p.m.	Night task digging (pairs to do 65 cubic feet in 2 hours).	
			Officers' Ride.	
			Camp fatigues.	
			Rifle slings, clinometers, prismatic compasses and stationery received.	
	18	7 a.m.	Physical drill.	
		9 a.m.	Infantry instruction in task digging.	
			Experiments on blowing down of barbed wire conducted.	
		2 p.m.	Officers' Ride.	
		7.30 p.m.	Night entrenchments (Task digging).	
	19	7 a.m.	Physical drill.	
		9 a.m.	Infantry instruction in task digging.	
			Barbed wire experiments continued.	

1577 Wt.W10791/1773 500,000 1/15 D. D. & L. A.D.S.S./Forms/C. 2118.

Army Form C. 2118.

WAR DIARY
or
INTELLIGENCE SUMMARY.
(Erase heading not required.)

Instructions regarding War Diaries and Intelligence Summaries are contained in F. S. Regs., Part II. and the Staff Manual respectively. Title pages will be prepared in manuscript.

Place	Date	Hour	Summary of Events and Information	Remarks and references to Appendices
Sutton Veny	April 19	2 p.m.	Officers' Ride.	
	20		2nd LIEUT. WILLCOCKS and 56 N.C.O.'s and men proceeded to CHRISTCHURCH for a Course of Pontooning.	
		7 a.m.	Physical drill.	
		9 a.m.	Experiments on barbed wire.	
			Camp orderly duties.	
		2 p.m.	Officers Ride.	
		7.30 p.m.	Night entrenchments and infantry instruction.	
	21	11 a.m.	Divine service.	
		9.30	Foot inspection.	
		p.m.	Forge and electric detonators received.	
	22	7 a.m.	Physical drill.	
		9 a.m.	Rifle, equipment and kit inspection.	
		10 a.m.	Harness and horse inspection.	
		11 a.m.	Rifle exercises.	
	23	11 a.m.	Divine service.	
			Camp fatigues.	

Army Form C. 2118.

WAR DIARY
or
INTELLIGENCE SUMMARY.
(Erase heading not required.)

Instructions regarding War Diaries and Intelligence Summaries are contained in F. S. Regs., Part II. and the Staff Manual respectively. Title pages will be prepared in manuscript.

Place	Date	Hour	Summary of Events and Information	Remarks and references to Appendices
Sutton Veny.	April 24.	7 a.m.	Physical drill.	
		9 a.m.	Use of grenades.	Ath
		2 p.m.	Bayonet fighting.	
		2.15.	Officers Ride.	
		9.30 a.m.	Infantry instruction.	
	25.	7 a.m.	Physical drill.	
		9 a.m.	Demolitions (electric).	Ath
		2 p.m.	Extension of working parties.	
		8 p.m.	Infantry instruction.	
			Two pontoon wagons and 19 drivers whips received.	
	26.	7 a.m.	Physical drill.	Ath
		9 a.m.	Mining and task digging (infantry instruction).	
			Camp fatigues.	
			33 G.S. bicycles received and 3 mettometers.	
	27.	7 a.m.	Physical drill.	
		9 a.m.	Spars, gyns, sheers, derricks, swinging derricks.	Ath

1577 Wt.W10791/1773 500,000 1/15 D. D. & L. A.D.S.S./Forms/C. 2118.

Army Form C. 2118.

WAR DIARY
of
INTELLIGENCE SUMMARY.
(Erase heading not required.)

Instructions regarding War Diaries and Intelligence Summaries are contained in F. S. Regs., Part II. and the Staff Manual respectively. Title pages will be prepared in manuscript.

Place	Date	Hour	Summary of Events and Information	Remarks and references to Appendices
Sutton Veny	April 27	2 p.m.	Bayonet fighting.	M.
	28		Cartridges, ball, .303, mark VII. 20,000 rounds received.	
		7 a.m.	Physical drill.	
		9 a.m.	Earthworks.	
		8.30 p.m.	Night operations, consolidation of trenches and infantry instruction.	M.
		4 p.m	Pay parade.	
		6.30 p.m.	Foot inspection.	
	29	7 a.m.	Physical drill.	M.
		10 a.m.	Mounted section parade with vehicles.	
			Camp fatigues.	
	30	10.45 a.m.	Church Parade.	M.

1577 Wt. W10791/1773 500,000 1/15 D.D.&L. A.D.S.S./Forms/C. 2118.

APPENDIX "A".

60th (LONDON) DIVISIONAL ENGINEERS.

3/3rd LONDON FIELD COMPANY. ROYAL ENGINEERS.

PROGRAMME OF WORK FOR WEEK ENDING 1st APRIL 1916.

MONDAY, 27th.	7.30 - 8.	Physical drill.	R.E. CAMP.
	9. 0 -12.30.	Earthworks & Mining.	SUTTON VENY TRENCHES.
	2. 0 - 4.	Earthworks.	do.
		Lecture on Demolitions.	R.E. CAMP.
		Camp orderly duties.	do.
TUESDAY, 28th.	7.30 - 8.	Physical drill and saluting drill.	do.
	9. 0 - 4.	Earthworks.	SUTTON VENY TRENCHES.
		Pontooning.	LONGLEAT PARK.
WEDNESDAY, 29th.	7.30 - 8.	Physical drill and saluting drill.	R.E. CAMP.
	9.30 - 12.30.	Earthworks, tripwires & automatic alarms.	SUTTON VENY TRENCHES.
	2. 0 - 4.	Earthworks and practical demolitions.	do.
THURSDAY, 30th.	7.30 - 8.	Physical drill and saluting drill.	R.E. CAMP.
	9.30 - 12.30.	Route march and road reconnaissance.	SUTTON VENY, CROCKERTON GREEN, LONGBRIDGE DEVERILL, SUTTON VENY. Map 122, Scale 1/63360.
		Camp orderly duties.	R.E. CAMP.
FRIDAY, 31st.	7.30 - 8.	Physical drill and saluting drill.	do.
	9. 0 - 12.30.	Earthworks & Mining.	SUTTON VENY TRENCHES.
	2. 0 - 4. 0.	Earthworks and practical demolitions.	do.
SATURDAY, 1st.	7.30 - 8.	Physical drill and saluting drill.	R.E. CAMP.
	9. 0 - 10.	Bayonet fighting.	do.
	10.0 - 12.	Kit inspection, squad and section drill.	do.

D R I V E R S.

D A I L Y.	Stables -	6.30 a.m.
	Riding and driving drill	9. 0 - 12 noon.
	Stables -	12 noon - 12.45 p.m.
	Exercising spare horses	2. 0 - 3. 0 p.m.
	Harness cleaning -	3. 0 - 4. 0 p.m.
	Evening stables -	4.30 p.m.

R.E. Camp,
Sutton Veny.
22nd March 1916.

APPENDIX "B".

60th (LONDON) DIVISIONAL ENGINEERS.

3/3rd LONDON FIELD COMPANY. ROYAL ENGINEERS.

PROGRAMME OF WORK FOR WEEK ENDING 8th APRIL 1916.

MONDAY, 3rd.	7.30 - 8. 0.	Physical drill.	R.E. CAMP.
	9. 0 - 12.30.	Earthworks & Mining.	SUTTON VENY TRENCHES.
	2. 0 - 3. 0.	Company drill. (Drivers attend).	R.E. CAMP.
	8.30 - 12. 0.	Night operations: Demolitions, flares & automatic alarms.	SUTTON VENY TRENCHES.
TUESDAY, 4th.	7.30 - 8. 0.	Physical drill and saluting drill.	R.E. CAMP.
	9. 0 - 4. 0.	Earthworks.	SUTTON VENY TRENCHES.
		Pontooning.	LONGLEAT PARK.
WEDNESDAY, 5th.	7.30 - 8. 0.	Physical drill and saluting drill.	R.E. CAMP.
	9. 0 - 4. 0.	Earthworks, demolitions and automatic alarms.	SUTTON VENY TRENCHES.
		Camp orderly duties.	R.E. CAMP.
THURSDAY, 6th.	7.30 - 8. 0.	Physical drill and saluting drill.	R.E. CAMP.
	9. 0 - 4. 0.	Earthworks.	SUTTON VENY TRENCHES.
	9. 0 - 10.0.	Knotting & Lashing.	R.E. CAMP.
	11.0 - 3.30.	Route march and road reconnaissance.	SUTTON VENY, KNOOK, CORTON, SUTTON VENY, Sheet 122. Scale 1" - mile.
FRIDAY, 7th.	7.30 - 8. 0.	Physical drill and saluting drill.	R.E. CAMP.
	9. 0 - 4. 0.	Earthworks & demolitions.	SUTTON VENY TRENCHES.
SATURDAY, 8th.	7.30 - 8. 0.	Physical drill and saluting drill.	R.E. CAMP.
	9. 0 - 10.0.	Bayonet fighting.	do.
	10.0 - 12.0.	Kit inspection; squad and section drill.	do.
		Camp orderly duties.	do.

D R I V E R S.

DAILY.	Stables	6.30 a.m.
	Riding and driving drill	9. 0 - 12 noon.
	Stables	12 noon - 12.45 p.m.
	Exercising spare horses	2. 0 - 3. 0 p.m.
	Harness cleaning	3. 0 - 4. 0 p.m.
	Evening stables	4.30 p.m.

RE. Camp,
Sutton Veny.
30th March 1916.

APPENDIX "C".

60th (LONDON) DIVISIONAL ENGINEERS.

3/3rd LONDON FIELD COMPANY. ROYAL ENGINEERS.

PROGRAMME OF WORK FOR WEEKENDING 15th APRIL 1916.

MONDAY, 10th.	7.30 - 8.	Physical drill.	R.E. CAMP.
	9. 0 - 12.30.	Earthworks & Mining.	SUTTON VENY TRENCHES.
	2.30 - 3.30.	Company drill. (Drivers attend).	R.E. CAMP.
	8.30 - 12.	Night operations: Earthworks and entanglements.	SUTTON VENY TRENCHES.
TUESDAY, 11th.	7.30 - 8.	Physical drill and saluting drill.	R.E. CAMP.
	9. 0 - 4.	Earthworks, demolitions & entanglements. (Camp orderly duties).	SUTTON VENY TRENCHES. R.E. CAMP.
WEDNESDAY, 12th.	7.30 - 8.	Physical drill and saluting drill.	R.E. CAMP.
	9. 0 - 4.	Pontooning (details).	LONGLEAT PARK.
	9. 0 - 4.	Spar bridging.	CAMP FIELD.
THURSDAY, 13th.	7.30 - 8.	Physical drill and saluting drill.	R.E. CAMP.
	9.0 - 10.15.	Knotting & lashing.	do.
	11.0 - 3.30.	Route march and road reconnaissance. By Sections.	SUTTON VENY, BISHOPSTOW, NORTON BAVANT, HEYTESBURY, SUTTON VENY. Sheet 122. Scale 1" - mile.
FRIDAY, 14th.	7.30 - 8.	Physical drill and saluting drill.	R.E. CAMP.
	9. 0 - 4.	Earthworks and demolitions. Camp orderly duties.	SUTTON VENY TRENCHES. R.E. CAMP.
SATURDAY, 15th.	7.30 - 8.	Physical drill and saluting drill.	R.E. CAMP.
	9. 0 - 10.	Kit inspection.	do.
	10.0 - 11.	Bayonet fighting.	do.
	11.0 - 12.	Company drill. (Drivers attend).	do.

DRIVERS.

DAILY.	Stables	6.30 a.m.
	Riding & driving drill	9.0 - 12 noon.
	Stables	12 noon - 12.45 p.m.
	Exercising spare horses	2. 0 - 3. 0 p.m.
	Harness cleaning	3. 0 - 4. 0 p.m.
	Evening stables	4.30 p.m.

R.E. Camp,
Sutton Veny.
5th April 1916.

APPENDIX "D".

60th (LONDON) DIVISIONAL ENGINEERS.

3/3rd LONDON FIELD COMPANY. ROYAL ENGINEERS.

PROGRAMME OF WORK FOR WEEK ENDING 22nd APRIL 1916.

MONDAY, 17th.	7. 0 - 7.45.	Physical drill.	R.E. CAMP.
	9. 0 - 12.30.	Earthworks & Mining.	SUTTON VENY TRENCHES.
	9.30 - 12.30.	Infantry instruction.	do.
	7.30 - 10. 0.	Night entrenchments.	do.
		Camp orderly duties.	R.E. CAMP.
TUESDAY, 18th.	7. 0 - 7.45.	Physical drill.	do.
	9. 0 - 12.30.	Task digging and demolitions.	SUTTON VENY TRENCHES.
	9.30 - 12.30.	Infantry instruction.	do.
	7.30 - 10. 0.	Night entrenchments.	do.
WEDNESDAY, 19th.	7. 0 - 7.45.	Physical drill and saluting drill.	R.E. CAMP.
	9. 0 - 12.30.	Task digging and entanglements.	SUTTON VENY TRENCHES.
	9.30 - 12.30.	Infantry instruction.	do.
	7.30 - 10. 0.	Night entrenchments.	do.
THURSDAY, 20th.	7. 0 - 7.45.	Physical drill and saluting drill.	R.E. CAMP.
	9. 0 - 12.30.	Use of spars.	SUTTON VENY TRENCHES.
	9.30 - 12.30.	Infantry instruction.	do.
	7.30 - 10. 0.	Night entrenchments.	do.
		Camp orderly duties.	R.E. CAMP.
FRIDAY, 21st.	10.30 a.m.	Church Parade.	do.
	12. 0	Pay parade.	do.
SATURDAY, 22nd.	7. 0 - 7.45.	Physical drill and saluting drill.	do.
	9. 0 - 10. 0.	Kit inspection.	do.
	10.0 - 11. 0.	Bayonet fighting.	do.
	11.0 - 12. 0.	Company drill. (Drivers attend).	do.

DRIVERS.

DAILY.	Stables	6.30 a.m.
	Riding and driving drill	9. 0 - 12 noon.
	Stables	12 noon - 12.45 p.m.
	Exercising spare horses	2. 0 - 3. 0 p.m.
	Harness cleaning	3. 0 - 4. 0 p.m.
	Evening stables	4.30 p.m.

R.E. Camp,
Sutton Veny.
17th April 1916.

APPENDIX "E".

60th (LONDON) DIVISIONAL ENGINEERS.
3/3rd LONDON FIELD COMPANY. ROYAL ENGINEERS.

PROGRAMME OF WORK FOR WEEK ENDING 29th APRIL 1916.

MONDAY, 24th.	7. 0 - 7.45.	Physical drill.	R.E. CAMP.
	9. 0 - 12.30.	Use of grenades.	do.
	2. 0 - 4. 0.	Bayonet fighting.	do.
	7.30. - 10. 0.	Infantry instruction by night.	SUTTON VENY TRENCHES.
	2.15 p.m.	Officers Ride.	
TUESDAY, 25th.	7. 0 - 7.45.	Physical drill.	R.E. CAMP.
	9. 0 - 12.30.	Demolitions.	SUTTON VENY TRENCHES.
	2. 0 - 4. 0.	Extension of working parties.	R.E. CAMP.
	7.30 - 10. 0.	Infantry instruction by night.	SUTTON VENY TRENCHES.
WEDNESDAY, 26th.	7. 0 - 7.45.	Physical drill.	R.E. CAMP.
	7.30 - 10. 0.	Infantry instruction by night.	SUTTON VENY TRENCHES.
		Camp orderly duties.	R.E. CAMP.
THURSDAY, 27th.	7. 0 - 7.45.	Physical drill.	R.E. CAMP.
	9. 0 - 12.30.	Knotting, lashing and use of spars.	do.
	2. 0 - 3. 0.	Bayonet fighting.	do.
	2. 15 p.m.	Officers Ride.	
	3. 0 - 4. 0.	Use of grenades.	do.
	7.30 - 10. 0.	Infantry instruction by night.	SUTTON VENY TRENCHES.
FRIDAY, 28th.	7. 0 - 7.45.	Physical drill.	R.E. CAMP.
	9. 0 - 10. 0.	Rifle, kit and foot inspections.	do.
	11.0 - 3. 0.	Section route marches.	do.
SATURDAY, 29th.	7. 0 - 7.45.	Physical drill.	do.
		Camp orderly duties.	do.

DRIVERS.

DAILY.	Stables -	6.30 p.m.
	Riding and driving drill	9. 0 - 12 noon.
	Stables -	12 noon - 12.45 p.m.
	Exercising spare horses	2. 0 - 3. 0 p.m.
	Harness cleaning -	3. 0 - 4. 0 p.m.
	Evening stables	4.30 p.m.

R.E. Camp,
Sutton Veny.
23rd April 1916.

Army Form C. 2118.

WAR DIARY
or
INTELLIGENCE SUMMARY.
(Erase heading not required.)

Instructions regarding War Diaries and Intelligence Summaries are contained in F. S. Regs., Part II. and the Staff Manual respectively. Title pages will be prepared in manuscript.

RECEIVED BY
21 JUN 1916
T.F. RECORDS, LONDON

Place	Date	Hour	Summary of Events and Information	Remarks and references to Appendices
SUTTON VENY.	1916 May 1.	7 a.m. to 4 p.m.	Training carried out in accordance with Appendix "A". Equipment received: 160 fms. 2½" cordage; 8 prismatic compasses.	A.
	2.	do.	The Company found Regimental duties. Training carried out in accordance with Appendix "A". Two sappers and one pioneer transferred from 4/3rd London Field Coy. R.E. Equipment received: Differential tackle; Nosebags.	A.
	3.	7.30 p.m. to 10.30 p.m.	Training carried out in accordance with Appendix "A". 272 men from 181st Infantry Brigade under instruction in Task Digging.	A.
	4.	7 a.m. to 4 p.m.	Training carried out in accordance with Appendix "A".	A.

T./184. Wt. W708—776. 500000. 4/15. Sir J. C. & S.

Army Form C. 2118.

WAR DIARY
INTELLIGENCE SUMMARY
(Erase heading not required.)

Instructions regarding War Diaries and Intelligence Summaries are contained in F.S. Regs., Part II. and the Staff Manual respectively. Title pages will be prepared in manuscript.

Place	Date	Hour	Summary of Events and Information	Remarks and references to Appendices
SUTTON VENY.	1916 May 5.	7 a.m. to 4 p.m.	The Company found Regimental Duties. Training carried out in accordance with Appendix "A". 2nd LIEUT. H. WILLCOCKS and 44 N.C.O.'s and men returned from Pontooning Course, CHRISTCHURCH. Instruction of Infantry by night cancelled, owing to bad weather.	
	6.	do.	Training carried out in accordance with Appendix "A". LIEUT. R.D. WALKER proceeded to ALDERSHOT for Course in Mounted Duties. Authority: 60th (London) Division Orders No. 352 dated 25th April 1916). The rear party, consisting of 1 N.C.O. and 8 men returned from CHRISTCHURCH.	
	7.	9.30.a.m.	Church Parade.	
	8.	7 a.m. to 4 p.m. 9.15 a.m.	The Company found Regimental Duties. Training carried out in accordance with Appendix "B". 360 men from 181st Infantry Brigade under instruction in Task Digging.	

Army Form C. 2118.

WAR DIARY
or
INTELLIGENCE SUMMARY

(Erase heading not required.)

Instructions regarding War Diaries and Intelligence Summaries are contained in F. S. Regs., Part II. and the Staff Manual respectively. Title pages will be prepared in manuscript.

Place	Date	Hour	Summary of Events and Information	Remarks and references to Appendices
SUTTON VENY.	1916 May 8.	11 a.m. and 5.30 p.m.	1 Officer and 6 N.C.O.'s attended Lectures on Anti-gas measures of defence by Major J.A. Hewitt, R.A.M.C. (Authority: 60th London Division Order 381 dated 4th May 1916).	
		8 p.m.	304 men from 181st Infantry Brigade under instruction in Task Digging.	
	9.	7 a.m. to 12.30 p.m.	Training carried out in accordance with Appendix "B".	
		8.30 p.m. to 12 midnght.	Route march: LONGBRIDGE DEVERILL, SHEAR CROSS, PARSONAGE BARN, SUTTON VENY.	
		11 a.m.	6 N.C.O.'s and men attended Lecture on Anti-Gas Measure of Defence by Major J.A.Hewitt.	
			Equipment received: Whips, drivers, 11. Blankets, saddle, 24.	
	10.	7 a.m. to 4 p.m. 7.30 " to 10.30 p.m.	Training carried out in accordance with Appendix "B".	
		8 p.m.	228 men from 181st Infantry Brigade under instruction in Task Digging.	

Army Form C. 2118.

WAR DIARY
of
INTELLIGENCE SUMMARY.
(Erase heading not required.)

Instructions regarding War Diaries and Intelligence Summaries are contained in F.S. Regs., Part II. and the Staff Manual respectively. Title pages will be prepared in manuscript.

Place	Date	Hour	Summary of Events and Information	Remarks and references to Appendices
SUTTON VENY.	1916 May 10.		Equipment received: Bags, Armourers, 2. Blocks, brake, 34.	"
	11.	7 a.m. to 4 p.m.	The Company found Regimental Duties.	
			Training carried out in accordance with Appendix "B".	"
		9.15 a.m.	328 men from 181st Infantry Brigade under instruction in Task Digging.	
	12.	7 a.m. to 4 p.m.	Training carried out in accordance with Appendix "B".	"
			Equipment received: Spanners, armament. Artificers double ended $\frac{1}{2}" - \frac{3}{8}"$ 13. $\frac{3}{4}" - \frac{5}{8}"$ 12. Gloves, hedging, prs. 20.	"
	13.	7 a.m. to 12 noon.	Training carried out in accordance with Appendix "B".	"
			One driver transferred to 7th Provisional Field Coy. R.E. WEELEY.	

Army Form C. 2118.

WAR DIARY
or
INTELLIGENCE SUMMARY.
(Erase heading not required.)

Instructions regarding War Diaries and Intelligence Summaries are contained in F. S. Regs., Part II. and the Staff Manual respectively. Title pages will be prepared in manuscript.

Place	Date	Hour	Summary of Events and Information	Remarks and references to Appendices
SUTTON VENY.	1916 May 14.	8.45 a.m.	The Company found Regimental Duties. Church Parade.	
	15.	7 a.m. to 4 p.m.	Training carried out in accordance with Appendix "C".	
	16.	7 a.m. to 12.30 p.m.	Training carried out in accordance with Appendix "C". In addition the Company was exercised in Ceremonial Drill. Route march: BISHOPSTROW, NORTON BAVANT, SUTTON VENY. Reference O.S. Sheet 122. Scale 1" - 1 mile.	
		8.30 p.m. to 11 p.m.	Training carried out in accordance with Appendix "C".	
		8.30 a.m.-12.30 p.m. 8.30 p.m.-12.30 a.m.	96 men from 181st Infantry Brigade under instruction in entanglements.	
	17.	7 a.m. - 4 p.m.	The Company found Regimental Duties. Training carried out in accordance with Appendix "C".	
		8.30 a.m.-12.30 p.m. 8.30 p.m.-12.30 a.m.	96 men from 181st Infantry Brigade under instruction in entanglements.	

Army Form C. 2118.

WAR DIARY
or
INTELLIGENCE SUMMARY

(Erase heading not required.)

Instructions regarding War Diaries and Intelligence Summaries are contained in F. S. Regs., Part II. and the Staff Manual respectively. Title pages will be prepared in manuscript.

Place	Date	Hour	Summary of Events and Information	Remarks and references to Appendices
	1916 May			
SUTTON VENY.	18.	7 a.m.– 4 p.m. 8.30 a.m.–12.30 p.m. 8.30 p.m.–12.30 a.m.	Training carried out in accordance with Appendix "C". 96 men from 181st Infantry Brigade under instruction in entanglements.	
	19.	7 a.m.– 4 p.m. 8.30 p.m.– 12.30 a.m.	Training carried out in accordance with Appendix "C". 96 men from 181st Infantry Brigade under instruction in entanglements.	
	20.	7 a.m.– 12 noon.	The Company found Regimental duties. Training carried out in accordance with Appendix "C".	
	21.	8.45 a.m.	Church Parade.	
	22.	7 a.m.– 4 p.m. 8.30 a.m.–12.30 p.m.	Training carried out in accordance with Appendix "D". 96 men from 181st Infantry Brigade under instruction in entanglements.	

Army Form C. 2118.

WAR DIARY
or
INTELLIGENCE SUMMARY.
(Erase heading not required.)

Instructions regarding War Diaries and Intelligence
Summaries are contained in F.S. Regs., Part II.
and the Staff Manual respectively. Title pages
will be prepared in manuscript.

Place	Date	Hour	Summary of Events and Information	Remarks and references to Appendices
SUTTON VENY.	1916 May 22.		Draft of 2 sappers and 1 driver received from 4/3rd London Field Coy. R.E. ESHER. Lieut. H.T. CURTIS transferred from 1/6th London Field Coy. R.E. as from 8/5/16. Extract from 60th London Divisional Engineer Orders No.121, dated 22 May 1916.	
	23.	7 a.m. - 4 p.m.	The Company found Regimental duties. Training carried out in accordance with Appendix "D".	
	24.	7 a.m. - 4 p.m.	Training carried out in accordance with Appendix "D". Route March: Company left Camp 9.30 a.m. via SUTTON VENY CAMP POST OFFICE, CROCKERTON GREEN, B.M. 444, BUCKLER'S WOOD, B.M. 618. Road junction east of M. of HORNINGSHAM, B.M. 569, LONGBRIDGE DEVERILL. Arrived R.E. Camp, SUTTON VENY 2.20 p.m. (Ref: O.S. Sheet 122. Scale 1" - 1 mile).	
	25.	7 a.m. - 4 p.m.	The Company engaged on laying out Review Ground, NORTH FARM. (Ref: O.S. Sheet 122, sec.13C Scale 1" - 1 mile).	
	26.	7 a.m. - 6 p.m.	The Company found Regimental Duties. Divisional Training carried out in accordance with 60th London Divisional Engineer Orders No.126.	

T2134. Wt. W708—776. 500000. 4/15. Sir J.C. &S.

Army Form C. 2118.

WAR DIARY
or
INTELLIGENCE SUMMARY.
(Erase heading not required.)

Instructions regarding War Diaries and Intelligence Summaries are contained in F. S. Regs., Part II. and the Staff Manual respectively. Title pages will be prepared in manuscript.

Place	Date	Hour	Summary of Events and Information	Remarks and references to Appendices
	1916 May			
SUTTON VENY.	27.	7 a.m. - 12 noon.	Training carried out in accordance with Appendix "D".	
	28.	8.45 a.m.	Church Parade. LIEUT. R.D. WALKER returned from Course of Mounted Duties, ALDERSHOT.	
	29.	7 a.m. - 4 p.m. 6 p.m.	The Company found Regimental Duties. Training carried out in accordance with Appendix "E". Rehearsal of Ceremonial Parade by Dismounted Section.	
	30.	8.15 a.m.	The Company proceeded to NORTH FARM for rehearsal of Review by the G.O.C.	
	31.	11.30 a.m.	Inspection by H.M. THE KING at NORTH FARM.	

T2134. Wt. W708-776. 500000. 4/15. Sir J. C. & S.

"A"

60th (LONDON) DIVISIONAL ENGINEERS.

3/3rd LONDON FIELD COMPANY. ROYAL ENGINEERS.

PROGRAMME OF WORK FOR WEEK ENDING 27th MAY 1916.

MONDAY, 22nd.		7.0 - 7.45. Bayonet fighting.	R.E. CAMP.
		9.0 - 4.0. Earthworks, entanglements & bombing exercises.	SUTTON VENY TRENCHES.
	x	Mounted Section. 9.0 - 4.0. Riding and driving drill.	CODFORD DOWN.
TUESDAY, 23rd.		The Company will find Regimental Duties.	
		7.0 - 7.45. Physical drill.	R.E. CAMP.
		9.0 - 10.0. Bayonet fighting.	do.
		10.0 - 12.30. Spar bridging.	do.
		2.0 - 4.0. Extension of working parties.	do.
WEDNESDAY, 24th.		Divisional Route March.	
THURSDAY, 25th.		8.0 - 4.0. (Pontooning and (Rowing drill. (Knotting & splicing.	LONGLEAT PARK.
FRIDAY, 26th.		The Company will find Regimental Duties.	
		Divisional Trench attack.	
SATURDAY, 27th.		7.0 - 7.45. Physical drill.	R.E. CAMP.
		9.0 - 10.30. Kit inspection.	do.
		10.30 - 12.0. Company drill. (Drivers attend).	do.

Cyclists will parade three days during the week for instruction.

Signallers will practice daily from 7.0 - 7.45 a.m.

DRIVERS.

DAILY.	x	Stables -	6.30 a.m.
		Riding and driving drill	9.0 - 12 noon.
		Stables -	12 noon - 12.45 p.m.
		Exercising spare horses	2.0 - 3 p.m.
		Harness cleaning -	3.0 - 4 p.m.
		Evening stables -	4.30 p.m.

R.E. Camp,
Sutton Veny.
19th May 1916.

"B"

60th (LONDON) DIVISIONAL ENGINEERS.
3/3rd LONDON FIELD COMPANY. ROYAL ENGINEERS.

PROGRAMME OF WORK FOR WEEK ENDING 6th MAY, 1916.

MONDAY, 1st.	7. 0 - 7.45.	Physical drill.	R.E. CAMP.
	9. 0 - 12.30.	Earthworks.	SUTTON VENY TRENCHES.
	2. 0 - 4. 0.	Bayonet fighting & bombing exercises.	R.E. CAMP.
TUESDAY, 2nd.	7. 0 - 7.45.	Physical drill.	R.E. CAMP.
	9.15	Infantry instruction.	SUTTON VENY TRENCHES.
	4. 0	Clean arms parade.	R.E. CAMP.
		Camp orderly duties.	do.
WEDNESDAY, 3rd.	7. 0 - 7.45.	Bayonet fighting.	do.
	9. 0 - 12.30.	Use of grenades, knotting & lashing.	SUTTON VENY TRENCHES.
	7.30 - 10.30. p.m.	Earthworks.	do.
THURSDAY, 4th.	7. 0 - 7.45.	Physical drill.	R.E. CAMP.
	9. 0 - 12.30.	Earthworks.	SUTTON VENY TRENCHES.
	2. 0 - 4. 0.	Extension of working parties and bayonet fighting.	R.E. CAMP.
FRIDAY, 5th.	7. 0 - 7.45.	Physical drill.	R.E. CAMP.
	7.30 - 10.30 p.m.	Earthworks.	SUTTON VENY TRENCHES.
		Camp orderly duties.	R.E. CAMP.
SATURDAY, 6th.	7. 0 - 7.45.	Physical drill.	do.
	9. 0 - 10. 0.	Knotting & lashing.	do.
	10. 0 - 11. 0.	Bayonet fighting.	do.
	11. 0 - 12. 0.	Company drill (Drivers attend).	do.

DRIVERS.

DAILY.	Stables -	6.30 a.m.
	Riding and driving drill	9. 0 - 12 noon.
	Stables	12 noon - 12.45 p.m.
	Exercising spare horses	2.0 - 3.0 p.m.
	Harness cleaning -	3.0 - 4.0 p.m.
	Evening stables -	4.30 p.m.

R.E. Camp,
Sutton Veny.
28th April 1916.

60th (LONDON) DIVISIONAL ENGINEERS.
3/3rd LONDON FIELD COMPANY, ROYAL ENGINEERS.

PROGRAMME OF WORK FOR WEEK ENDING 13th MAY, 1916.

MONDAY, 8th.	7.0 – 7.45.	Physical drill.	R.E. CAMP.
	9.0 – 12.30.	Earthworks.	SUTTON VENY TRENCHES.
	2.0 – 4.0.	Extension of working parties.	R.E. CAMP.
	7.30 – 10.30.	Camp orderly duties.	do.
TUESDAY, 9th.	7.0 – 7.45.	Physical drill.	R.E. CAMP.
	9.0 – 12.30.	Use of spars. Spar bridging.	do.
	3.30 – 12 p.m.	Section route marches.	
WEDNESDAY, 10th.	7.0 – 7.45.	Physical drill.	R.E. CAMP.
	9.0 – 12.30.	Demolitions & bombing exercise.	SUTTON VENY TRENCHES.
	2.0 – 3.0.	Clean arms parade & Company drill. (Drivers attend.)	R.E. CAMP.
	3.0 – 4.0.	Bayonet fighting.	do.
	7.30 – 10.30.	Earthworks.	SUTTON VENY TRENCHES.
THURSDAY, 11th.	7.0 – 7.45.	Physical drill.	R.E. CAMP.
	9.0 – 12.30.	Earthworks.	SUTTON VENY TRENCHES.
	2.0 – 4.0.	Knotting & Lashing. Spar bridging. Camp orderly duties.	R.E. CAMP. do.
FRIDAY, 12th.	7.0 – 7.45.	Physical drill.	R.E. CAMP.
	9.0 – 4.0.	Pontooning. Spar bridging.	LONGLEAT PARK. do.
SATURDAY, 13th.	7.0 – 7.45.	Physical drill.	R.E. CAMP.
	9.0 – 10.0.	Kit & rifle inspection.	do.
	10.0 – 11.0.	Bayonet fighting.	do.
	11.0 – 12.0.	Company drill (Drivers attend).	do.

DRIVERS.

DAILY.		
Stables	–	6.30 a.m.
Riding and driving drill		9.0 – 12 noon.
Stables	–	12 noon – 12.45 p.m.
Exercising spare horses		2.0 – 3.0 p.m.
Harness cleaning	–	3.0 – 4.0 p.m.
Evening stables	–	4.30 p.m.

R.E. Camp,
Sutton Veny.
6th May 1916.

"D"

60th (LONDON) DIVISIONAL ENGINEERS.
3/3rd LONDON FIELD COMPANY, ROYAL ENGINEERS.

PROGRAMME OF WORK FOR WEEK ENDING 20th MAY, 1916.

MONDAY, 15th.	7. 0 – 7.45.	Physical drill.	R.E. CAMP.
	9. 0 – 4. 0.	Secs. 1 & 2. Spar bridging.	HENFORD MARSH.
		" 3 & 4. Entanglements and bombing exercises.	SUTTON VENY TRENCHES.
TUESDAY, 16th.	7.30 – 12.30.	Route march.	Route to be selected.
	8.30 – 11 p.m.	Wire entanglements and extension of working parties.	SUTTON VENY TRENCHES.
	✗ Mounted Section.	9.0 – 4.0 Riding and driving drill.	CODFORD DOWN. Ref. O.S. Sheet 123. Sec. "1C".
WEDNESDAY, 17th.	7. 0 – 7.45.	Physical drill.	R.E. CAMP.
	9. 0 – 12.30.	Splicing, knotting and lashing.	do.
	2. 0 – 4. 0.	Spar bridging. Camp orderly duties.	do. do.
THURSDAY, 18th.	7. 0 – 7.45.	Physical drill.	do.
	9. 0 – 4. 0.	Pontooning.	LONGLEAT PARK.
FRIDAY, 19th.	7. 0 – 7.45.	Physical drill.	R.E. CAMP.
	9. 0 – 12.30.	Demolitions and revetting.	SUTTON VENY TRENCHES.
	2. 0 – 3. 0.	Kit inspection.	R.E. CAMP.
	3. 0 – 4. 0.	Lecture: First Aid & use of field dressing by M.O.	do.
SATURDAY, 20th.	7. 0 – 7.45.	Physical drill.	do.
	10.0 – 12. 0.	Bayonet fighting and extension of working parties.	do.

The Company will find Regimental Duties.

DAILY. 8.45. a.m. Rifle inspection for both dismounted & mounted sections.

Cyclists will parade three days during the week for instruction.

D R I V E R S.

D A I L Y.	Stables –	6.30 a.m.
	Riding and driving drill	9. 0 – 12 noon.
	Stables –	12 noon – 12.45 p.m.
	Exercising spare horses	2. 0 – 3 p.m.
	Harness cleaning –	3. 0 – 4 p.m.
	Evening stables –	4.30 p.m.

✗ See above.

R.E. Camp,
Sutton Veny.
11th May 1916.

60th (LONDON) DIVISIONAL ENGINEERS.

3/3rd LONDON FIELD COMPANY, ROYAL ENGINEERS.

PROGRAMME OF WORK FOR WEEK ENDING 3rd JUNE 1916.

MONDAY, 29th.		The Company will find Regimental Duties.	
	7. 0 - 7.45.	Physical drill & gas helmet instruction.	R.E. CAMP.
	9. 0 - 12 noon.	Company drill. (Drivers attend).	do.
	2. 0 - 4. 0.	Extension of working parties and gas helmet instruction.	do.
TUESDAY, 30th.	7. 0 - 7.45.	Bombing exercises and gas helmet instruction.	do.
	9. 0 - 10. 0.	Company drill. (Drivers attend).	do.
	10.0 - 12. 0.	C.R.E.'s parade (dismounted).	do.
	2. 0 - 4. 0.	Bombing and wire entanglements.	SUTTON VENY TRENCHES.
WEDNESDAY, 31st.		Inspection.	
THURSDAY, 1st June.		The Company will find Regimental Duties.	
	7. 0 - 7.45.	Bombing exercises & gas helmet instruction.	R.E. CAMP.
	9. 0 - 10. 0.	Bayonet fighting.	do.
	10.0 - 4. 0.	Revetting.	do.
X	Mounted Section. 9.0 - 4.0.	Riding and driving drill.	CODFORD DOWN.
FRIDAY, 2nd.	7. 0 - 7.45.	Physical drill.	R.E. CAMP.
	9. 0 - 3 p.m.	Spar bridging.	do.
	3. 0 - 4. 0.	Instruction in use of gas helmets.	do.
SATURDAY, 3rd.	7. 0 - 7.45.	Physical drill.	do.
	9. 0 - 10.30.	Kit inspection.	do.
	10.30 - 12 noon.	Company drill.	do.

Signallers will practice daily from 7.0 - 7.45 a.m.

DRIVERS.

DAILY.	Stables -	6.30 a.m.
	Riding and driving drill	9. 0 - 12 noon.
	Stables -	12 noon - 12.45 p.m.
	Exercising spare horses	2. 0 - 3. 0 p.m.
	Harness cleaning -	3. 0 - 4. 0 p.m.
	Evening stables -	4.30 p.m.

R.E. Camp,
Sutton Veny.
27th May 1916.

C O N F I D E N T I A L.

WAR DIARY

OF

3/3rd LONDON FIELD COMPANY, R.E.

from 1st June 1916, to 21st June 1916.

RECEIVED BY
21 JUN 1916
T.F. RECORDS, LONDON

Army Form C. 2118.

WAR DIARY
INTELLIGENCE-SUMMARY.
(Erase heading not required.)

Instructions regarding War Diaries and Intelligence Summaries are contained in F. S. Regs., Part II. and the Staff Manual respectively. Title pages will be prepared in manuscript.

Place	Date	Hour	Summary of Events and Information	Remarks and references to Appendices
SUTTON VENY.	1916 June 1.	7 a.m. - 4 p.m.	The Company found Regimental Duties. 2 Officers and 76 men proceeded on "Final Leave". (Authority: Headquarters letter A/1333/62, dated 30/5/1916. Equipment received: Cases, saw, hand, 4.	1.
	2.	7 a.m. - 3 p.m. - 3 p.m. - 11 p.m. - 11 p.m. - 7 a.m.	The Company engaged on excavations for Battalion Headquarters Dug Out, at SUTTON VENY Trenches. A draft consisting of 3 drivers and 14 sappers received from 4/3rd London Field Coy. ESHER.	2.
	3.	do.	Work continued on Battalion Headquarters Dug Out, SUTTON VENY Trenches. Equipment received:- Traces, saddlery, pairs, 6.	3.
	4.	8.45 a.m. 7 a.m. - 3 p.m. - 3 p.m. - 11 p.m. - 11 p.m. - 7 a.m.	Church Parade. Work continued on Battalion Headquarters Dug-Out, SUTTON VENY Trenches. 2 Officers and 76 men proceeded on Final Leave.	4.

T2134. Wt. W708—776. 500000. 4/15. Sir J. C. & S.

Army Form C. 2118.

WAR DIARY
INTELLIGENCE SUMMARY.
(Erase heading not required.)

Instructions regarding War Diaries and Intelligence Summaries are contained in F.S. Regs, Part II. and the Staff Manual respectively. Title pages will be prepared in manuscript.

Place	Date	Hour	Summary of Events and Information	Remarks and references to Appendices
SUTTON VENY.	1916 June 5.	7 a.m. —) 3 p.m. —) 3 p.m. —) 11 p.m. —) 11 p.m. —) 7 a.m.)	Work continued on Battalion Headquarters, Dug Out, SUTTON VENY Trenches. Equipment received:- Casks, water, R.E., 4.	Ah.
	6.	do.	Work continued on Battalion Headquarters Dug Out, SUTTON VENY Trenches. Mobilization Store Table, A.F. G.1098-114 dated May 1916 received.	Ah.
	7.	do.	Work continued on Battalion Headquarters Dug Out, SUTTON VENY Trenches.	Ah.
	8.	do.	Work continued on Battalion Headquarters Dug Out, SUTTON VENY Trenches. Capt. A.H.D. MONCRIEFF, O.C., proceeded on leave. 2 Officers and 84 other ranks proceeded on Final Leave.	Ah.
	9.	do.	Work continued on Battalion Headquarters Dug Out, SUTTON VENY Trenches.	Ah.
		10.30 a.m.	Brigadier-General C.H. BRIDGE, Inspector of Remounts, inspected the horses and mules of the Company.	

O.C. 2/1 LONDON FIELD Co. R.E.

Army Form C. 2118.

WAR DIARY
INTELLIGENCE SUMMARY.
(Erase heading not required.)

Instructions regarding War Diaries and Intelligence Summaries are contained in F. S. Regs., Part II. and the Staff Manual respectively. Title pages will be prepared in manuscript.

Place	Date	Hour	Summary of Events and Information	Remarks and references to Appendices
SUTTON VENY.	1916 June 10.	7 a.m. —) 3 p.m. —) 3 p.m. —) 11 p.m. —) 11 p.m. —) 7 a.m. —)	Work continued on Battalion Headquarters Dug Out, SUTTON VENY Trenches.	
	11.	do. 9.45 a.m.	Work continued on Battalion Headquarters Dug Out, SUTTON VENY Trenches. Church Parade.	
	12.	7 a.m. —) 3 p.m. —) 3 p.m. —) 11 p.m. —) 11 p.m. —) 7 a.m. —)	Work continued on Battalion Headquarters Dug Out, SUTTON VENY Trenches. Equipment received:- Boxes, candle, 12. Capt. MONCRIEFF, O.C., two Officers and 84 men returned from "Final Leave".	
	13.	do.	The Company found Regimental duties. Work continued on Battalion Headquarters Dug Out, SUTTON VENY Trenches.	
	14.	do.	Work continued on Battalion Headquarters Dug Out, SUTTON VENY Trenches.	

O.C. 2/3RD LONDON FIELD Co. R.E.

Army Form C. 2118.

WAR DIARY
or
INTELLIGENCE SUMMARY.
(Erase heading not required.)

Instructions regarding War Diaries and Intelligence Summaries are contained in F. S. Regs., Part II. and the Staff Manual respectively. Title pages will be prepared in manuscript.

Place	Date	Hour	Summary of Events and Information	Remarks and references to Appendices
SUTTON VENY.	1916 June 15.		Instructions received for the seven days programme, as ordered in Divisional Headquarters letter No.A/2363 dated 29/4/16, to come into force. (Authority 60th London Divisional Engineers letter No. 1889/R/16 dated 14-6-16.)	Ah
		7 a.m.– 4 p.m.	The first day's programme carried out in accordance with above.	
	16.	do.	The Company found Regimental Duties.	
			The second day's programme in accordance with above quoted instructions was carried out.	Ah
			The Company engaged in practice of throwing live bombs, at Divisional Bombing School.	
	17.	do.	The third day's programme carried out in accordance with Divisional Headquarters letter.	
			Lieut. R.D. WALKER admitted to Military Hospital, SUTTON VENY.	Ah
	18.	8.45.a.m.	Church Parade.	
			The fourth day's programme in accordance with Divisional Headquarters letter was duly carried out.	Ah
			2nd Lieut. A.O. BROWN was transferred to 3/3rd LONDON FIELD COMPANY, R.E. as from 17/6/16. (Authority: 60th London Divisional Engineers Ord rs No.146, part II, para.2c.)	

O.C. 3/3rd LONDON FIELD Co. R.E.

Army Form C. 2118.

WAR DIARY
of
INTELLIGENCE-SUMMARY.

(Erase heading not required.)

Place	Date	Hour	Summary of Events and Information	Remarks and references to Appendices
SUTTON VENY	1916 June 18.		Lieut. R.D. WALKER transferred to Third Line. (Authority: London District, No.6524A, dated 17.6.16.) Equipment received:- Wheels, wagon, pontoon, 1. Officers saddlery, sets, 1.	AM
	19.	7 a.m. & 4 p.m.	Programme carried out in accordance with Divisional Headquarters letter quoted under the 15th inst.	AM
	20.	do.	Programme carried out in accordance with Divisional Headquarters letter quoted under the 15th inst.	AM
	21		The 3/3rd LONDON FIELD COMPANY, R.E. proceeded overseas. Strength: Officers: 7. Other ranks: 211.	AM

O.C. 3/3rd LONDON FIELD Co. R.E.

Vol I

CONFIDENTIAL.

WAR DIARY of

3/3rd. LON. FIELD COY. R.E.

for the period

21st. to 30th. JUNE 1916.

Army Form C. 2118.

WAR DIARY
or
INTELLIGENCE SUMMARY.
(Erase heading not required.)

Instructions regarding War Diaries and Intelligence Summaries are contained in F.S. Regs., Part II. and the Staff Manual respectively. Title pages will be prepared in manuscript.

Place	Date	Hour	Summary of Events and Information	Remarks and references to Appendices
	1916			
WARMINSTER.	JUNE 21	A.M. 12-3	3/3rd LONDON FIELD COY. R.E. together with H. of E. Driver and Groom attached entrained for SOUTHAMPTON.	Mc
SOUTHAMPTON.	21	P.M. 6.0	COMPANY embarked in S.S. "CITY OF DUNKIRK". Strength :- OFFICERS 7. OTHER RANKS 212 (Including A.S.C.) 79 ANIMALS	Mc
HAVRE	22	A.M. 2.0	Arrived at HAVRE, disembarked 7 a.m. & proceeded to No. 1. (RAILWAY REST CAMP) Interpreter HENRI JAQUES LECOQ reported for duty.	Mc
Do	23	—	EXTRACT LONDON GAZETTE "Captain A.H.D.MONCRIEFF to be MAJOR, appointment dated 6TH MAY 1916.	Mc
Do	"	P.M. 11.40	COMPANY entrained for ST POL. Strength 7 OFFICERS 211 OTHER RANKS (With Interpreter) 79 ANIMALS. (1) No 2737 LANCE CORPL. FRANCIS proceeded to the A.G. OFFICE at ROUEN to be attached for duty. & (2) Left behind 1 (one) SAPPER in HOSPITAL.	Mc
ST. POL.	24	P.M. 3.30	DETRAINED. Casualty. One MULE lost off Railway train during Journey.	Mc
NEUVILLE-AU-CORNET	"	5-30	COMPANY arrived.	Mc
Do	25	P.M. 3.0	6 OFFICERS, 161 OTHER RANKS, the G.S. Wagon, A.S.C. Wagon & Cooks Cart left for LOUEZ, the remainder of the COMPANY remaining at NEUVILLE-AU-CORNET under Lieut JAMESON.	Mc
LOUEZ	"	P.M. 11.30	The COMPANY arrived at LOUEZ, and were billeted at the SUGAR REFINERY, the TRANSPORT and Horses at DOUISANS.	Mc
Do	26	—	COMPANY rest at LOUEZ.	Mc

Army Form C. 2118.

WAR DIARY
or
INTELLIGENCE SUMMARY.
(Erase heading not required.)

Instructions regarding War Diaries and Intelligence Summaries are contained in F.S. Regs., Part II. and the Staff Manual respectively. Title pages will be prepared in manuscript.

Place	Date	Hour	Summary of Events and Information	Remarks and references to Appendices
LOUEZ	1916 JUNE 27	4.0 P.M.	Captain CURTIS admitted to HOSPITAL.	
Do	"		COMPANY moved to ANZIN, the TRANSPORT remaining at DOUISANS.	
			The COMPANY is attached to the 51st (HIGHLAND) DIVISION, R.E. for Instruction.	
ANZIN	"		On arrival at ANZIN the Sections were allotted as follows:—	
			No 1 to MAISON BLANCHE, Nos 3 & 4 to ECURIE & No 2 to ROCLINCOURT. Head-Quarters to ANZIN.	
Do	28		Sections employed on INSTRUCTIONAL WORK under 51st DIVN. in Trenches, 3 N.C.Os & 10 Sappers employed in R.E. Yard.	
Do	29		COMPANY employed as above.	
Do	30		Ditto. Received 10. Gas Helmets.	

Confidential.

Copy
WAR DIARY

of the

3/2nd London Field Coy

Royal Engineers

1st – 31st July 1916.

Map Reference - Lens 11.

WAR DIARY - COPY -

Army Form C. 2118.

Place	Date 1916	Hour	Summary of Events and Information	Remarks and references to Appendices
ANZIN	July 1		Company employed under instruction of the 51st (Highland) Divn on the Right Sector of the XVII Corps area. Captain CURTIS discharged from 6th Stat. Hospital reports for duty. Lieut. JAMESON with 50 O.R. 50 Animals & 15 Vehicles arrives at MAROEUIL from LE TERLET.	
do	2		Company employed as above. Transport & animals moved from DOULLENS to MAROEUIL. Nos 2 & 4 Sections return to billets in ANZIN.	
do	3		Company employed as previous day.	
do	4		do	
do	5		do	
do	6		do	
do	7		H.N.C.O. & 2 Sappers stationed at Bois de Bray for work under O/C Light Rlys. 1 Sapper, in addition to above, proceeds to Bois de Bray.	
do	8		Lieut JAMESON returns from MAROEUIL to ANZIN.	
do	9		Company employed as previous day.	
do	10		do	
do	11		do	
do	12		Interpreter LECOCQ admitted to Hospital. Operation Order No 1 received. 3361 Spr Thomas G.H. wounded. 20 Steel Helmets received. Attached for instrns': Brigade Bombing Corporal. (1 N.C.O. 7 A.S's 1/8th Lond Regt) Major Moncrieff attended conference at ETRUN. 150 Steel helmets received. Sections (a 3 return billets in Anzin	
do	13	10 am	1/2nd Highland Field Coy R.E. (51st Divn) leaves ANZIN. TRENCHES & R.E. WORKS taken over from the 51st (Highland) Divn & usual certificates given. Billets of the 1/51st also taken over. ATTACHED to discipline & rations 9 men 7/22 2/7 Argyll & Sutd Highrs all 1/5 London Regiment. Attached to rations only 26 men of the 2/30 th Army Troops Coy. R.E. C.R.M.S. & Q.M. Stores moved from MAROEUIL to ANZIN. Confidential letter A/38/47 (DAQMG XVII Corps) dated 13/7/6 re Zeppelin Raids received.	
do	14		Four sections employed on FRONT LINE TRENCHES (Sectors L & M) improving & repairing same. ATTACHED for rations 1 N.C.O. & 2 Men (1/23 Bn Lond Regt) Bath attendants at ANZIN	
do	15		Company employed as above. Conference at ANZIN re R.E. Stores. Staff Capt Edwards attended. Fine, clear	
do	16		Company employed as previous day. Attached for discipline & rations 8 men 2/1 B London Regt. Fine	

N Curtis Capt
O.C. 1/2nd London Field Coy R.E.

Army Form C. 2118.

COPY
WAR DIARY
-or-
INTELLIGENCE SUMMARY.
(Erase heading not required.)

Instructions regarding War Diaries and Intelligence Summaries are contained in F. S. Regs., Part II. and the Staff Manual respectively. Title pages will be prepared in manuscript.

Place	Date 1916	Hour	Summary of Events and Information	Remarks and references to Appendices	Weather
ANZIN	July 17		Company employed as previous day. No. 2134 Sapper Brightman W.M. killed (2 Infantry of same party killed)	N/C	Hazy-rain at intervals.
do	18		Company employed as previous day. Sapper Brightman buried. Lt Jameson & 2 N.C.Os. leave for Gas Lectures at TREVIN CAPELLE.	N/C	Hazy & overcast.
do	19		Company employed as previous day. Attached to rations: 2 men of 230th Army Troops Coy. R.E.	N/C	Fine.
do	20		Company employed as previous day. Brigade Relief take place. 12 officers & O.R. of 1st INDIAN FIELD SQUAD? R.E. report at ANZIN & are billeted. CRE accompanied by G.S.O/1 inspects trenches.	N/C	Fine.
do	21		Company employed as previous day. Attached for rations:- 6 men 230th Army Troops Coy. R.E.	N/C	Fine.
do	22		Company employed as previous day. Gas Cylinders: Army No 6/23450 Gas Shells: Q/2/17 Purchase of bread	N/C	Fine.
do	23		Company employed as previous day. C.R.E. visits ANZIN	N/C	Fine.
do	24		Company employed as previous day.		Fine.
do	25		Company employed as previous day.		Fine.
do	26		Company employed as previous day. C.R.E. accompanied by Maj Muncrieff & Bgde Trench Mortar Officer visits trenches	N/C	Fine, cloudy.
do	27		Company employed as previous day. Received 1st by Bgde Order No 9 (secret)		Fine.
do	28		Company employed as previous day. Brigade Reliefs take place. Att'd for rations 2 men 230th A.T.Co. R.E. Casualty:- Horse (bay gelding) died.		Fine.
do	29	2.30pm	Company employed as previous day. Working party at F11 & F12 (GRAND COLLECTEUR) had a shell burst amongst them. 6 hty casualty. Attached for rations 6 men 230th Army Troops Coy. R.E.	N/C	Fine.
do	30		Company employed as previous day. Water supply in advanced trenches, improvements commenced. Adjutant accompanied by O.C. & Col Curtis visit forward dumps.		Fine
do	31		Company employed as previous day. Received in place of Casualty One L.D. Horse - Bay Gelding from Mob. Vet Lines at CABARET-BLANC.		Fine.

No 3, 3rd LONDON FIELD Co. R.E.

Army Form C. 2118.

WAR DIARY
or
INTELLIGENCE SUMMARY.
(Erase heading not required.)

Vol 3

Confidential

War Diary
of
3/3rd London Field Coy. R.E.

August 1916

WAR DIARY
or
INTELLIGENCE SUMMARY.
(Erase heading not required.)

Army Form C. 2118.

Instructions regarding War Diaries and Intelligence Summaries are contained in F.S. Regs., Part II. and the Staff Manual respectively. Title pages will be prepared in manuscript.

Place	Date	Hour	Summary of Events and Information	Remarks and references to Appendices
	1916			
ANZIN	AUG-1	PM PM 10.0 - 4.0	COMPANY employed on IMPROVEMENT and MAINTAINANCE of TRENCHES and INSTALLATION of TRENCH-WATER SUPPLY. Weather Fine and Very Warm – Wind S to SE	
Do.	" 2	do	COMPANY employed as on previous day. Weather Cloudy by day clearing later	
Do.	" 3	do	Ditto. Received 181st Infty Brigade Order No 10 (SECRET)	
			LIEUT: J.H. GARDNER- INDIAN-FIELD-SQUADRON-R.E attached for duty (Authority – 60 DIVL ENGRS-LETTER R Q/21/8 dated 2.8.16). Weather Fine & Dry	
Do.	" 4	do	C.R.E. accompanied by MAJOR. MONCRIEFF visits WATER-SYSTEM. REINFORCEMENT:- 4 Sappers from No 49 BASE-DEPÔT. HARFLEUR. Weather Fine, Cloudy later	
			COMPANY employed as on previous day CASUALTY:- No 2230 Sppr SAVERS (Shell Shock)	
Do.	" 5	do	COMPANY employed as on previous day. 181st INFTRY BRIGADE carry out Battalion Reliefs. Weather Fine	
Do.	" 6	do	COMPANY resting with the exception of men employed on WATER-SUPPLY + RE-YARD. Weather Fine	
			II- LIEUT. H.H. WHYTE proceeds to CRATER-CONSOLIDATION SCHOOL at AGNIERES	
Do.	" 7		COMPANY. resting. Deepening of Front Line Trenches terminated. Weather overcast clearing later	
Do.	" 8		Do some ft men employed on Water Supply and Yard	
			No 1954. Sergt CATER. G.G. proceeds to CRATER-CONSOLIDATION-SCHOOL at AGNIERES. Attached for Discipline (Infantry Fatigues) 41 of 2/22nd, 15 of 2/23rd + 31 of 2/24th Batns LOND-REGTS-(all Other Ranks)	
		P.M. 6.0	COMPANY resume work on Dugouts in the Supports + Water Supply. Weather fine Cloudy later	

Army Form C. 2118.

WAR DIARY
or
INTELLIGENCE SUMMARY.
(Erase heading not required.)

Instructions regarding War Diaries and Intelligence Summaries are contained in F. S. Regs., Part II. and the Staff Manual respectively. Title pages will be prepared in manuscript.

Place	Date	Hour	Summary of Events and Information	Remarks and references to Appendices
	1916			
ANZIN	Aug. 9		COMPANY employed on DUG-OUTS and WATER-SUPPLY. RECEIVED from DADOS Bags Nose 4, 6 Nets Hay 20 Ropes Head 14	Mw
	" 10		ATTACHED for Duty 5 other ranks 2/23rd Bth LOND-REGT. RETURNED to their UNIT. 8 other ranks 2/21st Bath LOND-REGT.	Mw
			Weather Fine.	
Do	" 11		COMPANY employed as on previous day.	Mw
			REINFORCEMENT. ONE Sapper from N.º 49 Depôt HARFLEUR ATTACHED for Duty. 18 other Ranks 2/21st Bn LOND-REGT + Rations	Mw
			Weather Fine. Some Rain.	
Do	" 12		COMPANY employed as on previous day. Weather fine, Heavy mist. later.	Mw
Do	" 13		Ditto. N.º 2176 Spr SHAW J. proceed. to III ARMY. COOKERY. SCHOOL at ST POL (Authority III ARMY AC/4582)	Mw
			Weather. Heavy Mist clearing during forenoon.	
Do	" 14		COMPANY employed as on previous day. 181.ST INFTRY-BRIGADE Carry out Battalion Reliefs	Mw
			Attached for Duty 21 other Ranks 2/21st LOND-REG.T. 4 20 of 2/23rd Bth LOND-REGT. Returned to their UNITS.10 of the 2/22 + 31 of 2/24 LOND. REGT.	
			Weather. Rain in early morning, fine later.	
Do	" 15		COMPANY employed as on previous day. 4 Sappers detailed to instruct. INFANTRY-TRENCH WARDENS (Authority H.Q. G 108/1/ddt 13.8.6)	Mw
			Received from DADOS 238 P.H.D. Gas Helmets. Weather fine, with Heavy Showers at intervals	
Do	" 16		COMPANY employed as on previous day of Aerial Bombs moved from L.2.0 Weather showery Wind WSW	Mw
			Ditto Weather Showery Wind WSW	Mw

[signature]

Army Form C. 2118.

WAR DIARY
or
INTELLIGENCE SUMMARY.

(Erase heading not required.)

Instructions regarding War Diaries and Intelligence Summaries are contained in F.S. Regs., Part II. and the Staff Manual respectively. Title pages will be prepared in manuscript.

Place	Date	Hour	Summary of Events and Information	Remarks and references to Appendices
	1916			
ANZIN	Aug 17		COMPANY employed as on previous day	NTC
			CASUALTY:- MAJOR MONCRIEFF to CASUALTY CLEARING STATION - No 42 at AUBIGNY	
"	" 18		Weather Showery	NTC
			COMPANY employed as on previous day	
			REINFORCEMENT One Sapper from No 49 Depot HARFLEUR. Received 181ST INFTRY BRIGADE ORDER - No 13 (SECRET) dec 19 7/2	
"	" 19		Weather Showery	NTC
			COMPANY employed as on previous day	
			MAJOR MONCRIEFF returns to duty Weather Showery	Mw
"	" 20		COMPANY employed as on previous day Weather fine	Mw
"	" 21		Ditto No 3 Section Resting 181ST INFTRY BRIGADE carry out Battn Reliefs	
			Attached for Duty 20 other ranks 2/23 + 31 of 2/24 Battn LOND REGT. Returned to UNITS 31 other Ranks 2/22 Bn LOND REGT	Mw
			Weather fine	
"	" 22		COMPANY employed as on previous day No 2 Section Resting 20 other Ranks 2/23 return to their Unit Weather fine	Mw
"	" 23		Ditto No 1 "	
			II LIEUT. NEIL & 48 other ranks 2/4TH LOND RE attached for Discipline + Rations	
		PM 10.0	SPECIAL WORK in FRONT LINE (see hors. Dw. Engrs No R R/367 - dted 23 7/8) Commenced Weather Showery Wind S.W	

WAR DIARY
or
INTELLIGENCE SUMMARY.
(Erase heading not required.)

Army Form C. 2118.

Place	Date	Hour	Summary of Events and Information	Remarks and references to Appendices
ANZIN	1916 AUG. 24		COMPANY employed on SPECIAL WORK in the FRONT-LINE Weather Fine Wind W.S.W.	
"	25		Ditto Ditto	
"	26		Ditto Weather Showery Wind SW - Rec'd. 181st Infty Brigade Order No 15 dated 21.8.16	
"	27		Ditto D° Wind SSE	
"	28		Ditto D° Wind SSW	
"	29		Ditto 181st BRIGADE carry out Battalion reliefs	
"			Attached for Duty 32 other ranks 2/22 Bn LOND-REGT. Returned to their UNITS 19 of 2/23 & 9 of 2/21 Bns LOND. REGT.	
"			Weather - unsettled - Thunder showers - Wind S.S.W.	
"	30		COMPANY employed as on previous day	
"			Attached for Duty 10 of the 2/24 LOND-REGT, & Returned to their Batt'n 10 of the 2/21st LOND. REGT.	
"			Weather - Heavy Showers Wind S.W. -	
"	31		COMPANY employed as on previous day	
"			CASUALTIES:- N° 2235 Spr COTTRELL W.H. (Gunshot) N° 2035 Spr PARKINS J.W. (Shell Shock)	
"			LIEUT J.H GARDNER, INDIAN FIELD-SQUAD, R.E. returns to AGNIERES	
"			Weather Fine Wind W.N.W	

CONFIDENTIAL.

WAR DIARY of 3/3rd. LONDON FIELD COY. R.E.
60th. LONDON DIVISIONAL ENGINEERS

for 1st. to 30th. SEPTEMBER, 1916.

Army Form C. 2118.

WAR DIARY
or
INTELLIGENCE SUMMARY.
(Erase heading not required.)

Instructions regarding War Diaries and Intelligence Summaries are contained in F.S. Regs., Part II. and the Staff Manual respectively. Title pages will be prepared in manuscript.

Place	Date 1916	Hour	Summary of Events and Information	Remarks and references to Appendices
ANZIN	Sept. 1		COMPANY employed on SPECIAL WORK in BONNAL Front line. This work completed. 1 Lt M&L 1 45 OTHER RANKS return to MAROEUIL. 1st INDIAN FIELD SQUADRON leave ANZIN. Weather Fine Wind S.W.	
Do	" 2		Received 151st Infantry Brigade Order No. 16 (SECRET) 2/9/16. Weather fine Wind S.W. overcast later.	
Do	" 3		COMPANY RESTING. Weather Fine Wind South.	
Do	" 4th		COMPANY RESTING.	
Do	" 5th		COMPANY EMPLOYED on Dug Outs in Front Line, Fitting Gas Frames, Trench Maintenance, Water Supply, etc. 181st Infantry Brigade carries out Batn. Reliefs. And for Discipline 30 O.R., 10 O.Rs (ALL OTHER RANKS) Weather fine Wind S.W.	
Do	" 6		COMPANY EMPLOYED as on previous day. Casualty Capt. Curtis admitted to Hospital. J.F. Ruffes joins as INTERPRETER. 10 men 2/2L returned to their Unit.	
	" 7th		COMPANY employed as on Previous Day and upkeep of Communication Trenches in ANZIN TRENCH, BIDOT & WICK AVENUES. 40 Special Fatigue provided for R. former & 20 for each of the latter. 1/Lt: Whyte returned to Duty. Weather fine Wind Easterly	
Do	" 7th		COMPANY employed as on Previous Day. Attd. for rations one other rank 147th Army Troop Company (R.E.) Weather fine. Wind N.E. 181st Infantry Brigade Order No. 18 (Secret, 8/9/16) received.	
Do	" 8th		COMPANY EMPLOYED as on Previous Day. C.R.E. visits Trenches with O/C 93rd? Weather fine Wind N.E.	
Do	" 9th		COMPANY Employed as on Previous Day. Weather fine Wind N.E.	
Do	" 10th		COMPANY employed as on Previous Day, except Communication Trenches. Battalion Reliefs carried out. Attd. 20 O.R. 2/23, 21 O.R. 2/21st returned 18 O.R. 7/2nd Lond. Regt. Weather fine Wind N.W.	

Major, London Field Co. R.E.

Army Form C. 2118.

WAR DIARY
or
INTELLIGENCE SUMMARY.
(Erase heading not required.)

Instructions regarding War Diaries and Intelligence Summaries are contained in F. S. Regs., Part II. and the Staff Manual respectively. Title pages will be prepared in manuscript.

Place	Date 1916	Hour	Summary of Events and Information	Remarks and references to Appendices
ANZIN	Sept. 11th		COMPANY EMPLOYED as on previous Day. Ill Case 1 30 Other Ranks leave for Mt. St. Eloy for temporary attachment to the 1/6 Lond: R.E. Returned to the 1/6 Lond: R.E.	
Do	" 12th		COMPANY EMPLOYED as on previous day, also in Wick, Bidot, ANZIN, & other trenches. One NCO & 6 men from Convalescent Station attached for discipline & Rations	
Do	" 13th		COMPANY EMPLOYED as on previous Day. Reinforcements Two men from Base Depot. Sergt Letter 150 Little End Weather Cloudy - Rain at night. Wind N.W.	
Do	" 14th		COMPANY employed as on previous day. Sergt Letter 60 Th. Eng. S/su Highl. scot. No. 2795 Sapper Shaw returned from Boulogne - Rest-Camp. Weather over cast & inclined to be showery.	
Do	" 15th		COMPANY employed as on Previous Day. Recd 151st Infantry Brigade No. 19 - 14 Or. Weather fine Wind N.W. veering N.	
Do	" 16th		COMPANY employed as on previous day. Battalion reliefs carried Out. 30 Other Ranks 2nd and 3rd disciplinary & duty & 20 2/Lieut. Ret to Bat no: 31 2/Lt & 10 Ors. 1st Goodyear But Atha & B's Ault HRH Mist & fine Wind N.	
Do	" 17th		Company employed as on previous day - working on four lines of trenches. R.E. Fatigues reduced to 10 men. A'Bath 20 'B'Bath & 30 'C' Bath. Weather fine, Cloudy storm towards Evening. Wind Veering N.	
Do	" 18th		Company Employed as on Previous Day. Weather Very Wet. Wind N.W.	
Do	19th		Company Employed as on previous day. Reinforcements Ten from Base Depot. Weather Showery	

WAR DIARY
or
INTELLIGENCE SUMMARY.
(Erase heading not required.)

Army Form C. 2118.

Place	Date 1916	Hour	Summary of Events and Information	Remarks and references to Appendices
ANZIN	Sept 20		COMPANY EMPLOYED as on previous day. Weather Showery. Wind N.W.	—
	21st		COMPANY Employed as on previous day. 181st Infantry Brigade No 20 road. Weather fine. Wind N.W.	21/9/16 —
	22nd		COMPANY EMPLOYED as on previous day. Battalion reliefs carried out. 2/22nd Batt. London Regt. Reld to Units 10 O/Rs + 20 o/siok. 10 otherranks 2/24 + 21. Weather fine. Wind N.	—
	23		COMPANY EMPLOYED as on previous day. 2/Lt CASE + 32 ORs. Ranks return from Mt St. Eloy. III Army School of Cookery Lt Goodyear 2/24 L. No: 3399 Sapper Razey. A.H. returns to his battalion. Weather fine. Wind N. Lond: Regt. returned to his battalion.	—
	24		Company employed as on Previous Day. Weather fine. Wind N.	—
	25th		COMPANY EMPLOYED as on Previous Day. Weather fine. Wind N.W.	—
	26th		COMPANY employed as on previous day. Attd for duty + rations Lt Robinson (Machine Gun Co) Reinforcement One - from No.11b Camp. Havre. Weather fine Wind W.	—
	27th		COMPANY employed as on previous day. Weather Fine. Wind N.W. 181st Infantry Brigade Order No8 received. Attd 10 men 2/22nd 2/23rd (OR+Ratns)	—
	28th		COMPANY employed as on previous day. Battalion reliefs carried out. Attd for duty + Ratns 2Lts Dowdall, Nurst + Weslow + 3 other ranks 2/22nd London Regt. Returned to Units 11 X + 2/21st. 10 x 2/24th Lond: Regt. Weather fine. Wind N.	—

Signature [illegible] MAJOR, 2/1st LONDON FIELD CO., R.E.

Army Form C. 2118.

WAR DIARY
or
INTELLIGENCE SUMMARY.
(Erase heading not required.)

Place	Date	Hour	Summary of Events and Information	Remarks and references to Appendices
ANZIN	1916 Sept 29th		COMPANY EMPLOYED as on previous day. Weather. Showery in morning, fine later. Wind N.E.	
Do	" 30th		COMPANY EMPLOYED as on previous day. Weather fine. Wind. N.E.	

Vol 5

Confidential

War Diary

of

3/3rd London Field Coy. R.E.

1st to 31st October 1916

Army Form C. 2118.

WAR DIARY
or
INTELLIGENCE SUMMARY.
(Erase heading not required.)

Instructions regarding War Diaries and Intelligence Summaries are contained in F.S. Regs., Part II. and the Staff Manual respectively. Title pages will be prepared in manuscript.

Place	Date	Hour	Summary of Events and Information	Remarks and references to Appendices
ANZIN	Oct. 1.		COMPANY employed on construction of DUGOUTS, TRENCH MAINTENANCE, WATER SUPPLY &c. Lieut ROBINSON (1818) Machine Gun Co.) returned to Unit. Reinforcement Lieut R.D. WALKER & Ill Lt FO STEPHENSON. Weather fine. Wind N.E.	Ab.
Do.	2		COMPANY employed as on previous day. Lieut WILLCOCKS returned from Special Works Park, WIMEREUX. 181st Infantry Bgde Order 11p 22 (Secret) received. Weather Wet. Wind W.	Ab.
Do.	3		COMPANY employed as on previous day. Weather showery. Wind N.W.	Ab.
Do.	4		COMPANY employed as on previous day. 181st Infantry Bgde carried out Battalion reliefs. Attached - 20. O.R. 7/23rd 11 O.R. 3/21st. 2nd Lieuts DOWDALL, HURST & WESTON of 4/22nd returned to their Battalion. Returned to their Units 10. O.R. 7/22nd 22 O.R. 7/24th Attached for rations Capt BRETT (Acting Town Major, ANZIN) & 1 O.R. 2/21st. Weather showery. Wind S.W.	Ab.
Do.	5		COMPANY employed as on previous day. Weather showery early morning, fine later. Wind S.W.	Ab.
Do.	6		COMPANY employed as on previous day. Weather wet. Wind S.S.W.	Ab.
Do.	7		COMPANY employed as on previous day. Weather wet. Wind S.W.	a.m.
Do.	8		COMPANY employed as on previous day. Weather showery. Wind S.W.	a.m.
Do.	9		COMPANY employed as on previous day. 181st Infy Bgde Order No 23 (Secret) received. Weather fine. Wind S.W.	a.m.
Do.	10		COMPANY employed as on previous day. 181st Infy Bgde carried out Battn reliefs. Attached 20. O.R. 7/24th 21. O.R. 7/23rd. Retd to their Units 22. O.R. 7/22nd 20. O.R. 3/23rd. Weather showery. Wind S.S.W.	a.m.
Do.	11		COMPANY employed as on previous day. Weather fine. Wind S.W.	a.m.

O.C. 520th LONDON FIELD Co. R.E.
Major.

Army Form C. 2118.

WAR DIARY
~~INTELLIGENCE~~ SUMMARY
(Erase heading not required.)

Instructions regarding War Diaries and Intelligence Summaries are contained in F.S. Regs., Part II. and the Staff Manual respectively. Title pages will be prepared in manuscript.

Place	Date	Hour	Summary of Events and Information	Remarks and references to Appendices
ANZIN.	Oct 12	—	COMPANY employed as on previous day. Weather fine. Wind. S.S.W.	M
Do	13		COMPANY employed as on previous day. Attachment to A.S.C. for H.Q. 60th Div. R.E. 1.O.R. Weather fine. Wind. S.S.W.	Ditto
Do	14		COMPANY employed as on previous day. Weather fine. Wind S.S.W.	Ditto
Do	15		COMPANY employed as on previous day. 102nd Infy.Bgde. Order No.24 (Secret) received. Weather showery. Wind N.W.	Ditto
Do	16		COMPANY employed as on previous day. 183rd Infy Bgde. carried out Battn. Reliefs. Att'd 22 O.R. 2/2nd 10 O.R. 2/4th Reg't to Their units. 20 O.R. 2/1st 10 O.R. 2/3rd Weather fine. Wind. N.N.W.	Ditto
Do	17		COMPANY employed as on previous day. Weather fine. Wind. N.W.	Ditto
Do	18		COMPANY employed as on previous day. Reinforcement 2 Sappers from No.1. Territorial Base Depot. Weather damp. Wind N.	Ditto
Do	19		COMPANY employed as on previous day. Weather very wet. Wind N.W.	Ditto
Do	20		COMPANY employed as on previous day. Weather fine. Wind N.W.	Ditto
Do	21		COMPANY employed as on previous day. All attached Infantry returned to their respective Units. 181st Infy Bgde Order No.25. (Secret) dated 21·10·16 received. 60th Div. Eng'r Order No.2. (Secret) dated 21st Oct/16 received together with amendments. Weather fine. Frosty. Wind N.E.	Ditto
Do	22		COMPANY employed as on previous day. Secret letter from 60th Div. H.Q. (unnumbered) dated 21·10·16 received. Weather fine. Wind N. Capt Maynard (O.C. 8th Canadian Field Co.) reported & was shown round workshops & works by O.C.	Ditto
Do	23	9 a.m.	COMPANY withdrawn from works. Works, Stores, R.E.Yard, M.T. & Billets handed over to 8th Canadian Field Co. & necessary receipts obtained. Amendment to 60th Div. Eng'r Order No.2 dated 21·10·16 received. Amendment to movement orders for 25·10·16 received from 181st Infy. Bgde.	Ditto
			Copy 60th Div. H.Q letter G.S. 3902/14 dated 23·10·16 received. Weather fine. Wind N.E. Advance party 8th Canadian Field Co. (1 Officer & 3 N.C.O's) reported.	

[signature] MAJOR
O.C. 520th LONDON FIELD Co. R.E.

Army Form C. 2118.

WAR DIARY
of
INTELLIGENCE SUMMARY.
(Erase heading not required.)

Instructions regarding War Diaries and Intelligence Summaries are contained in F.S. Regs., Part II. and the Staff Manual respectively. Title pages will be prepared in manuscript.

Place	Date	Hour	Summary of Events and Information	Remarks and references to Appendices
			MOVES. Map Reference :- Lens II. Scale 1/100,000.	
ANZIN.	Oct 24	9am	8 Officers 207 O.R. left & proceeded via MAREUIL, HERMAVILLE, IZEL-LES-HAMEAU to FERME DOFFINE.	
HERMAVILLE	"	Noon	Reinforcement 1 Lieut F.W. Head from Army Territorial Base Depot	
FERME-DOFFINE.	"	4 pm	9 Officers 207 O.R. arrived with Transport. Weather wet. Wind N.W.	
D°	25	9am	9 Officers 207 O.R. left & proceeded via AMBRINES, SARS-LES-BOIS, BERLENCOURT, ESTRÉE-WAMIN, BEAUDRICOURT to IVERGNY.	
IVERGNY	"	3.15pm	9 Officers 207 O.R. arrived. 60th Div. Eng's Order No. 3 dated 25-10-16 received, also Order No. 4 dated 25-10-16 received. Weather showery. Wind N.W.	
D°	26		COMPANY overhauling and refitting equipment. Weather wet. Wind S.W.	
D°	27		COMPANY employed as on previous day. 181st Inf'y Bgde Order No. 26 (Secret) dated 26-10-16 received. Weather wet. Wind S.W.	
D°	28	9.30am	9 Officers 199 Other Ranks left, with Transport. 6 O.R. remain in Hospital. 2 O.R. attached to 60th Div. Train. Route from IVERGNY via LE SOUICH, BOUQUEMAISON, NEUVILLETTE to OCCOCHES.	
OCCOCHES	"	(2.30pm)	9 Officers 199 Other Ranks arrived. 181st Inf'y Bgde Order No. 27 (Secret) received. Weather showery. Wind S.W.	
D°	"		Orders received (unnumbered) from 181st Inf'y Bgde to march to FAMECHON on 29th inst.	
D°	29	9.30am	9 Officers 199 Other Ranks left & proceeded via DOULLENS, BEAUREPAIRE, HALLOY, to HURTEBISE FARM, FAMECHON.	
FAMECHON.	"	2.30pm	9 Officers 199 Other Ranks arrived. Quartered at HURTEBISE FARM. Company attached to XIII Corps. Weather stormy. Wind S.W. Frosty.	
D°	30	9.0am	1 Officer 32 Other Ranks proceed to COIGNEUX. Remainder of Company resting. Wind S.W. Gusty. Showery.	
D°	31	10 am	7 Officers 119 Other Ranks left. 1 Officer + 50 Other Ranks and Transport (including A.S.C. Wagon & personnel att'd) remain at Hurtebise Farm. Route from FAMECHON via PAS, COUIN, to COIGNEUX	
COIGNEUX.	"	1.0pm	8 Officers 151 Other Ranks arrived. Weather showery. Wind S.S.W.	

WAR DIARY

OF

3/3rd. LONDON FIELD COMPANY. R.E. (T)

NOVEMBER 1916.

CONFIDENTIAL

Army Form C. 2118.

WAR DIARY
of
INTELLIGENCE SUMMARY.
(Erase heading not required.)

Instructions regarding War Diaries and Intelligence Summaries are contained in F.S. Regs., Part II. and the Staff Manual respectively. Title pages will be prepared in manuscript.

Place	Date	Hour	Summary of Events and Information	Remarks and references to Appendices
			MOVES:- Map reference:- Lens 11., Abbeville 14., Amiens 17. Scale 1/100,000.	
COIGNEUX.	Nov. 1		Company employed under orders of C.E. XIII Corps.	
		11.30am.	1 Officer & 39 Other Ranks proceeded via Couin & Pas to Famechon (Hortebise Farm). Weather cold & Wet. Wind. S.W.	Ah—
Do.	2	8.45am.	7 Officers & 113 Other Ranks proceeded by 6 Motor Buses via Authie, Mairieux, Surtan & Doullens, to Outrebois.	Ah—
OUTREBOIS.		11.30am.	7 Officers & 113 Other Ranks arrived, from Coigneux.	
		3.30pm.	2 Officers 99 Other Ranks and transport arrived from Famechon. Route via Doullens.	
			Reinforcement of 2 Other Ranks received from No. 1. Territorial Base Depot. Weather Showery. Wind. S.W.	Ah—
Do.	3	8.45am.	9 Officers & 202 Other Ranks together with Transport (less A.S.C.) proceeded via Autheux, Fienvillers & Bernevil to St. Hilaire.	
SAINT HILAIRE.		1.p.m.	9 Officers & 202 Other Ranks arrived. Weather fine. Wind S.W.	Ah—
Do.	4		Promotion:- II Lieut. R.C. Case to be Temp'y. Lieut. Antedated 15-8-1916. Authority- London Gazette 2.11.1916.	Ah—
		10.40 a.m.	7 Officers & 132 Other Ranks proceeded to Brucamps, together with transport.	
		4 pm	1 Officer & 30 Other Ranks proceeded to Bettangles & attached to 14th Wing Royal Flying Corps.	
			1 Officer & 36 Other Ranks proceeded to Allonville & attached to 3rd Wing Royal Flying Corps. Weather fine. Wind. S.W.	
			Tool & Forage cart taken by each detachment.	
BRUCAMPS.	5	1.20pm	7 Officers, 132.Other Ranks & Transport arrived.	
Do.			Company employed overhauling & cleaning wagons & equipment. Major A.H.D Moncrieff, O.C. proceeded to	Ah—

Army Form C. 2118.

WAR DIARY
INTELLIGENCE SUMMARY.

(Erase heading not required.)

Instructions regarding War Diaries and Intelligence Summaries are contained in F. S. Regs., Part II. and the Staff Manual respectively. Title pages will be prepared in manuscript.

Place	Date	Hour	Summary of Events and Information	Remarks and references to Appendices
BRUCAMPS	Nov 5		England on leave. Authority:- C.R.E. War Establishment Part XII Salonika 4th 1916 received, also 181st Infy. Base letter A/6/1293/2. Programme of Adjustment of Transport &c; and 2 letters from C.R.E. No. R.Q.486 of 4-11-16. Weather showery. Wind S.W.	Am
Do	6	9.30 am.	Conference at C.R.E's office, A/O.C. (Lieut Walker) attended. Company training, handling of arms, spent at rifle digging. 1 Other Rank returned from BERTANGLES. II Lieut Whyte & 30 Other Ranks proceeded on leave to England. Authority:- C.R.E. Transfer. 1 Cooks Cart complete less driver exchanged with H.Q. 60th Div A.S.C. Train for 1- G.S. Wagon complete less driver. Weather fine. Wind S.W.	Am
Do	7		Company employed cleaning & preparing equipment for overseas & transport for return to Ordnance. 30 Bicycles returned to D.A.D.O.S.	Am
		7. p.m.	1- Officer & 29 Other Ranks returned from BERTANGLES by motor car.	
		8. p.m.	1- Officer & 36 Other Ranks returned from ALLONVILLE by motor car. Weather showery. Wind S.W.	
Do	8		72 Other Ranks proceeded to DOMART to bath as ordered by 181st Infy Bgde. Company employed as on previous day. 1- G.S. Wagon, 8 Tool Carts & 2 R.E. Limbered Wagons returned to A.H.T. Depot A.S.C. Weather wet. Wind. S.W.	Am
Do	9		Company employed as on previous day. II Lieut Stephenson & 1.O.R. attended lecture on Box Respirators at 181st Infy. Bgde H.Q. 22 L.D. Horses returned to 2nd Indian Cavalry Res. Park & 22 Mules received in exchange. Weather fine. Wind. S.W.	Am
Do	10		Company employed as on previous day. Reinforcement of 20 Other Ranks (Mounted) arrived from No. 4 Gen. Base Depot. 3 Riders received from Remount Depot, ABBEVILLE. 19 Mules returned to No. 4 Coy A.S.C. Weather fine. Wind S.W.	Am

[Signature] MAJOR
O.C. 3/3rd LONDON FIELD CO. R.E.

Army Form C. 2118.

WAR DIARY
INTELLIGENCE SUMMARY.

(Erase heading not required.)

Instructions regarding War Diaries and Intelligence Summaries are contained in F. S. Regs., Part II. and the Staff Manual respectively. Title pages will be prepared in manuscript.

Place	Date	Hour	Summary of Events and Information	Remarks and references to Appendices
BRUCAMPS.	Nov 11		Company employed as on previous day. 95% of Coy inoculated T.A.B by M.O 2/22nd Batt Lond. Regt Draft of 22 Mounted & 6 dismounted O.R received from No 1 Territorial Base Depot & No 4 Genl Base Depot. All animals malleined for glanders. Authority letter S/V 24/13 dated 8-11-1916. 61 Lane. A.D.V.S. 60th Divn. One Mule rejected & handed over to Mobile Vety. Section. Weather fine. Wind S.W.	AM
Do	12		Company employed preparing transport to hand over to Hqrs R.E. Completion of inoculation of Company. 2 Lieut Whyte returned from leave. Weather fine. Wind. S.W.	AM
Do	13		Company training. Squad drill, handling of arms, use of Box Respirator. 15 Drivers transferred to Hq. R.E. Water Cart handed to A.H.T. Depot No1 Section, A.S.C., 2 Pontoon, 1-Trestle, & 2 R.E. Limbered Wagons handed over to 2/4th Lond. Field Coy at Faucourt sur Somme. Weather overcast. Wind S.W.	AM
Do	14		Company training - Route march. 3. O.R. returned from leave. 7. O.R. employed under C.E. XV Corps at Long. Authority: CR.Es letter R.Q 502 of 13-11-16. 1 Rider handed over to 1/6th Lond. Field Coy. R.E. 1-Mule & 2 sets wheel harness handed to 520th H.T. Coy. A.S.C. Letter R.Q.486 received notifying that Field Coys would receive orders from Brigade in future. Weather overcast. Wind N.E.	AM
Do	15		Company training. Major. A.H.D Moncrieff returned from leave. Weather fine, very cold. Wind N.E.	AM
Do	16		Company training. 100- O.R. bathed at DOMART. Weather fine, very cold. Wind N.E.	AM
Do	17		Company training. Weather fine, very cold. Wind S.E.	AM

Major
LONDON FIELD Co RE

WAR DIARY
INTELLIGENCE SUMMARY.

Army Form C. 2118.

Place	Date	Hour	Summary of Events and Information	Remarks and references to Appendices
BRUCAMPS.	Nov 18		Company training. Weather damp; very cold. Wind N.E.	Am
Do	19	11.30am	Company parade for Church. Weather dull; milder. Wind S.	Am
Do	20		Company training. Weather dull. Wind S.	Am
Do	21		Company training. Received letters G.S.104/1 & G.S.430 Forecast of moves &c. from 181st Infy Bgde. Weather fine; cold. Wind S.S.W.	Am
Do	22		Company training. Received letter G.S.104/2 from 181st Infy Bgde also G.S.431 (Cohy 20) Programme of Entrainment & Sch 'A' (Move Order) Weather fine; cold. Wind W.	Am
Do	23		Company training. Received letter A1611/79 from D.A.A.& Q.M.G. 'Programme for Nov 25th 1916' Weather fine; cold. Wind S.W.	Am
Do	24		Company training. 1-G.S Wagon 2-H.D. Horses & Harness P.D.G.S. handed to No1 A.S.C. Section A.H.T.D. 3 Bicycles returned to D.A.D.O.S. Weather fine; cold. Wind S.W.	Am
Do	25	8.30am	6 Officers 235 Other Ranks & 24 animals proceeded via VAUCHELLES to LONGPRE. Lieut J.F. Jameson, II Lt A.O. Brown, III Lt. F.W. Head & No 2099 Sp Harris F.T. left the Coy at BRUCAMPS (Surplus to War Estab t Fort XII Salonika "A" 1916)	Am
LONGPRE.		11.am	6 Officers 235 Other Ranks & 24 animals arrived.	
		11.30pm	6 Officers 235 Other Ranks & 24 animals entrained for MARSEILLES. Weather wet. Wind S.W.	

WAR DIARY

~~INTELLIGENCE SUMMARY~~

(Erase heading not required.)

Army Form C. 2118.

Instructions regarding War Diaries and Intelligence Summaries are contained in F.S. Regs., Part II. and the Staff Manual respectively. Title pages will be prepared in manuscript.

Place	Date	Hour	Summary of Events and Information	Remarks and references to Appendices
St Julien-du-Sault	Nov 26	6.15pm	Company in train en route for MARSEILLES. Collision with goods train.	An.
	27	6 p.m.	Company in train en route for MARSEILLES. Weather fine. Wind N.E.	An.
MARSEILLES	28		6 Officers 235 Other Ranks 24 animals detrained. 5 Officers & 212 O.R. proceeded to The Old Distillery, POINTE ROUGE. 1 Officer 23 O.R. & 24 animals proceeded to CAMP VALENTINE. Weather fine. Wind N.E.	An.
Do (Pointe Rouge)	29		Company resting. Weather fine. Wind N.E.	An.
Do	30	9.20am	5 Officers & 212 O.R. proceeded to CAMP MUSSO.	An.
CAMP MUSSO		10.10am	5 Officers & 212 O.R. arrived. Captain H.T. Curtis reported for duty. Authority:- Telegram of 60th Division H.Q. Weather fine. Wind N.E.	An.

Major

60TH DIVISION

60TH DIVL SIGNAL COY R.E.

~~NOV 1916~~

1915 OCT — 1915 DEC
1916 JUN — 1916 NOV

www.ingramcontent.com/pod-product-compliance
Lightning Source LLC
Chambersburg PA
CBHW081445160426
43193CB00013B/2390